Greenwood

Christian

Tatiana Goricheva

Talking about God is Dangerous

*The Diary of a
Russian Dissident*

CROSSROAD • NEW YORK

1989
The Crossroad Publishing Company
370 Lexington Avenue, New York, N.Y. 10017

Translated by John Bowden from the German
Von Gott zu reden ist gefährlich,
Meine Erfahrung im Osten und im Westen,
published 1985 by Herder Verlag,
Freiburg, Basel and Vienna

Printed in the United States of America

Library of Congress Cataloging-in-Publication Data

Goricheva, Tatiana.
Talking about God is dangerous.

Translation of: Von Gott zu reden ist gefährlich.
1. Goricheva, Tatiana.   2. Orthodox (Orthodox Eastern
Church)   3. Refugees, Political—Soviet Union—Biography.
4. Russkaia pravoslavnaia tserkov'—Soviet Union—
History—20th century.   5. Orthodox Eastern Church—
Soviet Union—History—20th century.   6. Soviet Union—
Church history—1917-   .   I. Title.
BX597.G618A3   1987   281.9'3 [B]   86-29328
ISBN 0-8245-0798-3

Contents

An Encounter with the Devil

Boris's visit

On 14 November at 8 o'clock in the morning our door bell rang. I had gone to bed late the night before, so I had only just woken up when my father called out,

'Tatiana, a visitor for you!'

'Who?'

'Boris.'

I raised my head and tried to recognize who was standing in the hallway. There was a large, black figure. When he saw that I was looking closely at him, he tried to hide in the shadows. The thought struck me that perhaps one of my Moscow friends had come. But the next thought was the right one: it was the KGB, the secret police.

I had not replied to the written summons from Investigator Karmazkii in connection with the Moscow seminar. The most important member of the seminar, Vladimir Poresh, had recently been arrested. Not long before that we had been discussing with Vladimir how we could combine our seminars in Leningrad and in Moscow. We had started to dream and had even arrived at the idea of an Orthodox underground academy, an academy in which Volodya would teach church history, Regelson would take over dogmatics and I would do philosophy. Now they are all in the gulag: Sasha Ogorodnikov, Volodya, Tanya Shchipkova, Vitya Popkov and Liova Regelson. And the arrests and house searches are still going on.

Since I had not obeyed its summons in the matter of Vladimir Poresh, the KGB had come in person. My sleepiness was gone in a flash. I was wide awake, and I went out to Boris.

'What right have you to be here?'

He quickly showed me his red card.

'Come on, Tatiana Mikhailovna; let's not make things more complicated. The car is waiting down below.'

He said all this in a whisper, so that my parents shouldn't hear.

'I'm not going anywhere with you.'

I sat down at my desk and began to read Karl Rahner's *Foundations of Christian Belief*.

When my parents understood what was going on they rushed up to me. What had I not told them?

'Go, if he's asking you nicely; otherwise you'll shame us in front of all the neighbours. They already take you for a nun. You've been studying for so long, and all to no avail.'

That was my mother getting worked up. When I went out of the house every day the poor dear hid my icons so that the neighbours shouldn't see them. She sighs and can't get to sleep when I pray in the bathroom in the evening, which is where I hide away from my parents.

'You're ready to hand me over to any number of bands of robbers,' I said. 'And the KGB is the worst of all.'

My parents walked up and down our home; they didn't know what to do or how they could influence me. All this time Boris stood quietly in the corridor, first on one foot and then on the other. They rushed up to him.

'Do sit down for a bit. Wouldn't you like some tea? See what a crazy girl she is.'

My mother, who is ashamed of me, whispered to him:

'She speaks three languages, she's read philosophy and has been singled out as having great promise. And she's not joined the party, and she has done something else. Just imagine, she's working as a lift attendant!'

Boris answered quite reasonably, 'That's her business...'

Just imagine that, the KGB acting as my moral advocate!

2

But my poor parents were out of their minds with anxiety and lack of understanding. They had always known that their daughter was unreasonable and stubborn, but this! Look at all the trouble the KGB had taken to get the crazy thing just to answer a few very simple questions! They had not only sent a Volga, but detached such a nice young man from his official duties. How good the KGB was not yet to have put this anti-Soviet fanatic in prison!

Anxiety was in my parents' blood, an anxiety which crippled any normal ideas and any healthy feelings. I kept quiet and didn't move. Finally Boris got impatient. 'Can one telephone from here?,' he asked.

'Do please telephone,' they replied in a duet of wheedling voices. 'We'll connect the telephone for you straightaway; we disconnect it overnight because there are so many calls.'

Boris talked to someone from the KGB.

'What, fetch her with the police? She won't go that way, and it's useless to come back again. Besides, it's so far away.'

'Call the police,' was the reply he got. And so Boris asked the police for a captain who had authority to take statements and 'can take down a declaration if Goricheva is prepared to make one'.

Here my parents' hysteria reached its climax.

'Don't give us a bad reputation with the neighbours,' my mother wept.

My father was quivering all over; he was about to have a nervous breakdown. A call came from the police; the car that had been asked for was on the way. I began to feel sorry for my father, and as in any case the armed police would succeed in taking me away, I got up and said that I was prepared to go.

At the KGB I was taken to Karmazkii who, dignity person-ified, introduced himself to me and gave me a paper to read on the rights and duties of witnesses.

'I refuse to take part in this business,' I said.

'Why? Can't you give us, say, a favourable characteriz-ation of your friend Poresh? We're not inhuman, and simply want to get everything clear. You know that you won't help him with your refusal, but you'll hurt yourself.'

'I refuse to talk to you.'

It wasn't the first time that I had been within these walls. At the beginning it was very difficult to find the right line to take with the KGB. The majority of those who are questioned there first begin by lying and invent something, make something up. But when it comes to cunning the devil is always cleverer than we are. Any dialogue at all with them is always a fool's game. Ultimately they discover what they need to know by cunning, well-tried and carefully worked-out methods, and people turn traitor.

When I was first brought within these walls about ten years ago and they began to question me about friends at the philosophy faculty, I tried to invent something or only say good things. But then when I got back home again I discovered to my dismay that the majority of the questions were trick questions, and were not meant to discover what they seemed to be asking about. So for example I was asked where V.F. lived, and I gave his address on the assumption that the KGB would discover it anyway. However, the investigator only wanted to know how well I knew V.F. And that's what always happens. They manipulated me, played with me. But this meeting was enough for me to work out the only possible tactic for dealing with the KGB: I simply refuse to talk to them. Later the KGB tried various psychological tricks to get me to join in a conversation. The strict investigator was replaced by a gentle one; I was

4

threatened with being stuck in a psychiatric clinic, and pressure was put on my parents. I tried to take no notice of all this.

'Believe nothing, be afraid of nothing, ask for nothing'

I prayed quietly for myself. The Jesus prayer in particular helped me: 'Lord Jesus Christ, Son of God, have mercy on me, a sinner.' This prayer created an impenetrable field around me. Thanks to this prayer I felt utterly protected, no matter what walls I was inside and in what circumstances I found myself.

The Holy Fathers recommend fighting demons by taking no notice of them, not allowing them into the faith. I tried the same method in warding off the persistent, extremely varied attempts of the KGB investigators which often went on for hours. I did not react to them. I did not allow them into my consciousness. So in our practice the experience of the dissidents and ascetical experience coincided. Solzhenitsyn had given a similar rule of thumb for coping with the KGB: 'Believe nothing, be afraid of nothing, ask for nothing.'

There was another obvious similarity between the procedures of this organization and the methods of the Evil One: how skilfully they exploit human weaknesses, the devilish sense of evil that they in fact have! Their existence is based on the exploitation of the lower human feelings: anxiety, envy, vanity, mistrust. When they note that something comes into being – seminars, newspapers, groups – they do not begin with arrests but attempt to destroy the new and living thing from within, stirring up people against one another, setting them at odds with one another. It was just the same with our religious seminars. The KGB people were particularly disturbed when they discovered that Baptists were coming to our seminar who belonged to groups which were not registered (and therefore were particularly persecuted). They invited these Baptists individually and tried to get them to explain what sort of people we are. They said that Father Lev Konin, an active member of the seminar, was a pervert. They said that I was a drunkard. And they said that others were thieves, prostitutes or layabouts. Our Baptists (who were even disturbed when people smoked in our seminar) had a highly developed moral feeling. So the KGB tried to impress them by putting us in an immoral light. But in conversations with us they called the Baptists 'grim fanatics', 'cruel and inhuman', 'agents of American espionage', and so on. Of course we saw through these tactics and laughed at them. They did not succeed in making us and the Baptists enemies. But the KGB was not always as clumsy as that.

'I refuse to speak to you.' This was the only thing that I said during my last visit to the KGB.

Karmazkii went out for ten minutes. During this time I sang to myself a familiar prayer, 'Dearest Lord Jesus'. As I knew how long one can sit with the KGB I had taken care to bring my hymn book from home.

When Karmazkii came back, he began another conversation with me. Clearly he had had instructions from his superiors. He tried me on an abstract topic.

'Tell me, Tatiana Mikhailovna, where did you and Poresh get such belief in God from? You were brought up in an ordinary Soviet family, your parents are intelligent people, atheists. You have no social roots in the faith. You don't come from the nobility or from the kulaks (peasants). Our society as a whole cannot produce any religious belief since we have no basis for it. There is no exploitation of people, there is atheistic propaganda everywhere, everyone can read and write and no one believes in fairy stories any more. We're all interested why you should believe. Why do you believe this nonsense, university people like you? Like any old woman who can't read or write?'

That's not the first time that the KGB tried such a basic conversation. At one time I would join in, explain how I could believe, try to make it clear that our faith could not be explained by any kind of Western influence, that the living God had come into my soul, that there is no greater joy than this new life in the church. I don't know whether I managed to communicate anything at all to them. I doubt it. Even now they carry on an inexorable battle with faith, with the Spirit, with that which is not accessible to their consciousness, with what they regard as the greatest threat to themselves and what they clearly regard as their most dangerous enemy – and they are murderers, cynics, inhuman and devilishly cunning. They found no 'materialistic' explanation for the Christian renewal in contemporary Russia. Nor will they find any. But that did not prevent them from condemning the deeply moral, gentle and gifted Volodya Poresh to eleven years imprisonment. Tatiana Shchipkova, who also spent years in prison, is now almost blind, and Sasha Ogorodnikov has become seriously ill.

And what can we do to help? We their friends who for the moment are still at liberty? I felt a burning shame that my love was so helpless. And so I shook my head when Karmazkii said, 'I'm asking you for the second time. Are you refusing to give evidence? You know your responsibilities under section 181?'

I shook my head, meaning, 'I know, I'm prepared.'

A room with rubber plants

I don't know how many years they give for refusing to make a statement. Probably one or two. But Volodya had to know that he has true friends.

However, that was not the end of my 'conversation' with the KGB. They took me through long corridors, all looking the same, with no pictures or writing whatsoever on the walls, with all the doors closed in the same dumb and inaccessible way: a world as cold as a nightmare. There was something unreal about it. This was the realm of evil, oppressive and mysterious.

For a whole hour they shut me in a room with sofas and

rubber plants. I prayed and wondered what made this time so difficult and why I felt so tense.

It may seem ridiculous, but the hardest experience among the things that I managed to bear over those hours was the prohibition against loving.

And how difficult that was! I had been living these last few years in a state of happiness, bliss. Someone – I think that it was Nikolai Berdyaev, wrote: 'Cross of freedom: freedom and the cross combine in one'; my life became an act of creation in God. This creating opened up to me the greatest, inexhaustible, incomparable source of joy. But one can only create by loving. And how simple it was then to see each person as the image and similitude of God, to be enthusiastic over bright, strong people, to suffer with those who were maltreated and experienced evil: 'to weep with those who weep and to laugh with those who laugh'!

But here in this world, where one might not become weak, where one is afraid, not for oneself but for the others, where one is afraid of harming one's friends if one is weak and gets drawn into a conversation – here one must be as 'gentle as a dove' but also 'as wise as a serpent'.

But how difficult that is! How hard it is to see a face in front of one which, however bloated, however expressionless, is nevertheless the face of a human being. A human being for whom our Lord God allowed himself to be crucified!

Yes, he too is a human being, and he has a Christian name!

The best thing, the only thing, is to remain silent.

Blessed is the one who does not walk in the counsel of the wicked

Finally they took me out of my room with the rubber plants and tried to draw me into another conversation. No use. This time I was not threatened. The KGB knows that that doesn't work with me. They tried to begin a conversation about philosophy, about my articles, about Heidegger. The investigator, who on the whole did not give the impression

8

of being a particularly educated person, had apparently prepared himself for the 'philosophical' conversation, had discovered who Heidegger was. But all to no avail. It was as though I was not there. The lines from the first psalm were running round in my head: 'Blessed is the one who does not walk in the counsel of the wicked.'

This visit to the KGB was one of many. Quite an average visit. The only unusual thing was that I had not been picked up on the street but that I had been taken from my home.

After this visit my father was taken into the hospital for war-wounded with inflammation of the thyroid gland. I could not live at home any more. One more visit like that, or – God forbid – a house search and the lives of my parents would be at risk. May God the Lord forgive me for having caused them so much suffering.

My Conversion

From nowhere to nowhere

When I am asked what turning to God meant to me, what I discovered through this conversion and how it has changed my life, I can give a very simple and short answer: everything. Everything has changed in me and around me. Or, to put it more precisely: my life only began when God found me.

For anyone who has grown up in the West that is difficult to understand. People in the West are born into a world in which there are traditions and norms, even if they are no longer quite stable. People can grow up 'normally', read the books that they want to, visit friends and plan a career. They can travel into other countries. Or they can withdraw from the world, either into a family where they can love one another and care for one another, or into a religious or academic community – wherever they want.

By contrast, I was born in a land from which the traditional values of culture, religion and morality had been deliberately and successfully eradicated; I was on a journey from nowhere to nowhere: I had no roots and would go into an empty, meaningless future. During my childhood I had a girl friend who committed suicide at the age of fifteen because she could no longer bear everything around her. She died and left a note, 'I'm a very bad person' – and yet she was someone with an unusually pure heart, who could not bear other people telling lies and could not tell lies herself. This girl committed suicide because she felt that she was not living as she should and that at some point one had to pierce through the surrounding emptiness and find light. But she could not find the way. My girl friend was too profound, and an extraordinarily conscientious person for her age; she understood that she too had a share of responsibility. Today, twenty years after her death, I can put it in Christian terms: she discovered her sinfulness. She discovered a fundamental truth, namely that human beings are weak and incomplete; but she did not find the other truth, which is still more important, that God can save human beings, lift them up out of their fallenness and snatch them out of the most impenetrable darkness. No one had told her anything about this hope, so she died, forced under by despair.

I hated everything and loved solitude

I was far inferior to my girl friend with all her gifts. I lived like a hunted, evil little beast, without ever standing up and raising my head, without making an attempt to understand anything or decide anything. In school essays I wrote the sort of thing that was expected, that I loved my country and Lenin and my mother – but all that was a glib lie. From childhood on I hated everything around me: I hated the people with their petty cares and anxieties, indeed they disgusted me; I hated my parents, who were the same as everyone else and just happened to be my parents. I seethed with rage when I thought how I had been brought into the world without wanting to be there and in a completely absurd way. I even hated nature with its eternal round and tedious rhythm: summer, autumn, winter...

The only thing that I loved was complete solitude. The time I liked best was when my parents were invited out and I could be all by myself in our little room. Then I began to dream – of mysterious fairy-tale castles and the infinite. Later, when I had learned to read, I used books as an impenetrable curtain to shield myself against the world. I was always deep in a book – on walks, during the lunch

11

hour, in breaks. The heroes of novels were courageous and free people, above everything, who did not yield to the deadly conformity of life. They were my ideal. But at that time I thought that such people were to be found only in books. Only in books did people not live in anxiety over being put at a disadvantage, deceived or robbed; only in books did people not live constantly with lies. Neverthless even as a child I quietly promised myself that I would be loyal to those crazy heroes who were not understood: the impetuous Cyrano de Bergerac or the lonely Ovid. Better to die than become an 'ordinary' person like everyone else.

However, the contempt there was within me did not prevent me from outwardly being an obedient and quiet child who regularly stood out as a result of particular achievements, a child whom her teachers praised and her friends envied. Of course I was not aware how inconsistent my behaviour was; my awareness and my conscience had not been aroused.

No one had told me that the supreme thing is to love

And school only encouraged our external, 'competitive' qualities. Praise at school is for those who can work better and rise higher, who 'distinguish' themselves in some way.

That served further to consolidate my pride and bring it to full bloom. My aim was to be cleverer, more capable, stronger than the others. But no one had told me that the supreme thing in life is not to overtake and to get the better of others, but to love. To love to the death, like the One, the Son of Man, whom at that time we did not yet know.

On the other hand there was constant talk of 'great deeds', of the heroic actions of the revolutionaries, of the iron will of the heroes of the War, like Maresiev, the man who could walk and dance without legs and whose name could only be read in bold type, or of the 'brilliant personality' of

12

Rakhmetov, who was ready 'to sleep on nails' for his ideas. So one had to develop a strong will, the will to conquer.

It is well known how many supporters of Nietzsche emerged from my generation, and indeed how many of them the nature of life in the Soviet Union still produces: passive supporters of Nietzsche, like Raskolnikov, the small 'hero of the underground', and also those who are very keen on rank and title and talk cynically of how we shall soon have conquered the whole world.

I read Nietzsche when I was nineteen (the gospel, though, only when I was twenty-six!!) and he seemed to me on first acquaintance to be very good – like Sartre, Camus, Heidegger, that 'existential' and rebellious philosophy which was so close to us. These writers were partly allowed during the years of liberalization under Khrushchev, and translations were circulated in the underground literature. In cafés and buses the intelligentsia discussed the question of a meaningless, contrary existence.

We were perhaps more enthusiastic about the 'idols' of the West than people are here in the West. For us existentialism was the first taste of freedom, the first public discussion that was not forbidden. It is interesting, though, that after that our ways soon parted. The youth of the West experienced the events of 1968 and took the course of an increasingly strong political awareness, becoming enthusiastic about Marxism; even now they live by the revolutionary myth.

By contrast we went into the depths and discovered the imperishable values of culture, history and ethics. Finally we turned to God and the church. Here in the West that has remained a quite incomprehensible development.

I do not want to praise 'us', as has already happened here and there. Nevertheless I sometimes have the impression that the Russian intelligentsia is more 'grown-up' than that in the West. Living in the West seems like being in the old Russia of the middle of the nineteenth century, when the

13

thought of the intellectual élite was dominated by the idea of revolution and a just society. Probably that does not happen when life is hard, but only when people get bored.

So our liberation began with the discovery of Western free thought.

Interestingly, once we came into contact with the wide and wonderful thought-world of Christianity we did not write off the godless Sartre and the haughty Camus. For all his hostility to religion Sartre could bring us to the verge of despair at which faith begins. His central idea, that human beings make a free choice every second, is indeed a Christian notion. For God wants the free love of human beings, and out of respect for our free decision he has not yet abolished even evil from the world.

Sartre led us to the Christ of the 'legend of the Grand Inquisitor', to the great tragedy of Christianity, the Christianity which makes human beings the bold offer that they can become children of God, friends of the Saviour and finally divine. Thus the Holy Fathers said, 'God became human to make human beings divine.' Sartre says, 'Human beings have no essence.' The only way in which they differ from stones or cabbages is that they are not programmed. With enormous joy we threw off the roles that had been imposed on us by society, the system, our anxieties and illusions. With enormous joy we purged spirit and soul of the clichés, the insipid myths and ideologies. It was as though within us we were preparing a room which only He could occupy; only He could fill the unfathomable depths of the abyss, because He himself had come to know and had conquered the deepest depths.

But I'm getting ahead of myself.

As a consistent and angry existentialist, for a long time I had nothing to do with Christianity. Why bring back the old myths? However, in my life there was a tendency towards increasingly great self-assertion and self-destruction. Following Nietzsche I regarded myself as an intellect-

14

ual aristocrat, i.e. as a 'strong' person, capable of directing and shaping my life simply by free decisions of my will. Ordinary 'weak' people could not bear this challenge from 'nothingness' and they ran away from the meaninglessness of being, some into family and others into politics or a career. Oh, how I hated them all, how well I knew how to 'enslave' people, then directly afterwards to point out maliciously that all of them, men and women, love slavery and in fact look for it.

I stopped telling lies

At that time I was already looking for a 'total', consistent way of life. I felt that I was a philosopher and stopped telling lies to myself and others. The bitter, fearful, sorry truth was more important to me than anything else. Nevertheless my existence was still divided and contradictory. I still delighted in contrast and the absurd, in the imponderables of life. I was also enamoured of aestheticism. For example I much enjoyed being a 'brilliant' student and the pride of the philosophical faculty; I enjoyed cultured conversation with sophisticated intellectuals, stood at the speaker's desk at academic conferences, made ironical comments and when it came to intellectual matters was satisfied only with the best. However, in the evenings and at night I kept company with outsiders and people from the lowest levels of society – thieves, psychological cases and drug addicts. I enjoyed this low atmosphere. We got drunk in cellars and attics. Sometimes we broke into a house, just for the fun of drinking a cup of coffee and then vanishing again.

Only one person tried to restrain me. I may rightly call him my first teacher. He was our professor Boris Mikhailovich Paramonov. He was only by chance a teacher in the faculty of philosophy and could not stand it for long. Now he is an emigrant and lives in America.

He once said to me, 'Tatiana, why are you trying to destroy everything? Don't you understand that this delight

15

in destruction has always been the bane of Russian thought? Look, we live in a world in which nihilism has already won a complete victory. You need only go into the Soviet market and you'll find empty counters everywhere. There's nothing to sell. Instead there are red banners everywhere, on which is written, 'Forward to the victory of Commmunism', 'One step forward and two back – Lenin', and so on. There you have the absurdity on which you're so keen. It's already been achieved by the Bolsheviks. Completely. What do you want to add?'

At the time these words made a deep impression on me. But neither Paramonov nor I knew then how to get out of this vicious circle and create life, instead of destroying it.

Nor did I find a way out of it in my enthusiasm for Eastern philosophies, in Yoga, with which I became occupied after my studies. Yoga merely opened up the world of the absolute to me, let my spiritual eye perceive a new vertical dimension of being and destroyed my intellectual arrogance. But Yoga could not free me from myself. Now I stopped living by my knowledge, culture or deliberate reflection, since I knew that there are unfathomable and unsuspected powers in human beings. I learned to deal in some way with the energies that I discovered in myself. Yoga teaches a convenient 'energetism', i.e. materialism, and there is nothing 'fairy-tale' about it. So for us unbelievers it became something like a small bridge between the empirical world and the transcendent world. Moreover it had a discipline that was very attractive to us: with the help of exercises and the knowledge of 'astral' and 'mental powers', with a great sense of purpose and awareness, one could become a superman. But why? Everyone answered this question as pleased them best. I wanted, of course, to become like a god. I wanted for myself everything that I had wanted before, but on a higher, spiritual level. I wanted to be the wisest and the strongest. In addition I also had feelings with a religious colouring. I wanted to be fused with the absolute and be steeped in eternal bliss. Now I had to fight against negative feelings like hatred or irritation, for I knew that they 'cost energy' and threw me back on a lower level of being. However, the emptiness which had long been my fate and which constantly surrounded me was not overcome. Indeed, it became even greater, became mystical, uncanny, disturbing to the point of madness.

An unbounded heaviness overcame me. I was tormented by incomprehensible, cold, hopeless anxieties. It was as though I were going mad. I did not want to live any longer.

How many of my former friends have become victims of this terrible void and have committed suicide! How many of them have become alcoholics! How many of them are in mental institutions! It seemed that we had no hope in life.

A second birth, my real one

But the wind which is the Holy Spirit 'blows where it wills'. It gives life and raises the dead. So what happened to me? I was born again. Yes, it was a second birth, my real one.

But all in due time.

I was doing my yoga exercise with the mantras wearily and without pleasure. I should point out that up to this point I had never said a prayer, nor did I know any. But in a yoga book a Christian prayer, the 'Our Father', was suggested as an exercise. The very prayer that Our Lord himself prayed. I began to say it as a mantra, automatically and without expression. I said it about six times, and then I was suddenly turned inside out. I understood – not with my ridiculous understanding, but with my whole being – that he exists. He, the living, personal God, who loves me and all creatures, who has created the world, who became a human being out of love, the crucified and risen God.

At that moment I understood and grasped the 'mystery' of Christianity, the new, true life. That was real, genuine deliverance. At this moment everything in me changed.

The old me died. I gave up not only my earlier values and ideals, but also my old habits.

Finally my heart was also opened. I began to love people. I could understand their suffering and also their lofty destiny, that they are in the image of God. Immediately after my conversion everyone simply seemed to me to be a miraculous inhabitant of heaven, and I could not wait to do good and to serve human beings and God.

What joy and what a bright light there was in my heart! And not only within me; no, the whole world, every stone, every shrub was bathed in a gentle light. The world became a royal, high-priestly garment of the Lord. How could I have overlooked that before?

So my life began. My deliverance was quite specific and real; it seemed surprising and yet I had long desired it, and only the Holy Spirit could bring it about in me because only he can make a 'new creation' and reconcile it with the Eternal. Only through him and his grace can the central conflict of human personality, the conflict between freedom and obedience, be resolved.

The Mystery of Reconciliation,
or My First Confession

I too belong to this 'people'

An enormous, cold church, gleaming white and very splendid. Six o'clock in the morning. The service will soon be beginning. In the left-hand aisle of the church a large and varied crowd of pilgrims has gathered. They include many women wearing simple, poor clothes, with scarves tied round their heads reaching right down to their eyebrows. Some of them come from a long way away: from the Ukraine, from Kazakhstan, from the remoteness of Siberia. These women have been preparing for months and years for their journey to the monastery, to the source of the Mother of God. They have put money aside, prayed, waited until despite the difficulties of a life laden with cares, they could realize the most secret desire of their soul: a journey to the monastery, to the holy places, to the profoundly wise priests known as the *startsy* (plural of *starets*), and the miraculous relics.

For months and years they have not been able to go to confession and to communion. Only a few churches are now left in the enormous expanses of Russia, and there are even fewer priests.

There are men here, too, also from the simple people, faces that one seldom comes across in the cities, but rather in the Russian villages; this kind of face has not disappeared from the depths of the countryside. It is as though it has come out of a picture by a nineteenth-century Russian painter. These people, clad in rags, now standing before the priest preparing them for confession with heads bent low in penitence, and as if turned to stone, caused me too, for the first time in my life, to say solemnly and with reverence that word which is so worn out by demagogues and misused the world over: 'people'. Only here in church did I understand what 'people' means. Only in God can the people really be people. And then at last it also became clear to me that now I am no longer alone, that I too belong to this people, because these unknown people were more akin to me than anyone else in the land.

Father Hermogen spoke gravely about sin. All who had gathered to make their confession wept silently. Just one man could not hold back his bitter sobbing, and his trouble and grief could be heard throughout the church. This pilgrim was clothed in very old rags; he had lost his right arm, and the left was amputated up to the elbow. Nevertheless, with the remaining stump of his left arm he made the sign of the cross in his own way; he crossed himself frequently and vigorously.

We knew virtually nothing

I had come to make my confession for the first time in my life. Shortly beforehand I had become a Christian by the grace of God. I had no deeper knowledge either of Christianity or of the church – who could have taught me? I and my newly-converted girl friend, both in the same position, learned what to do by imitating our old women, who zealously preserved the Orthodox faith and practices. We didn't know anything. But we had something which in our day should perhaps be treasured more than knowledge: a boundless trust in the church, belief in all its words, in every movement and demand. Only yesterday we had rejected all authority and all norms. Today we understood the deliverance that we had experienced as a miracle. We regarded our church as the indubitable, absolute truth, in minor matters just as much as in its main concern. God has

20

changed us and given us childhood: 'Unless you become as children, you will not enter into the kingdom of heaven.'

I only knew that it was necessary to go to confession and to communion. I knew that both confession and communion were high sacraments which reconcile us with God and even unite us with him, really unite us with him in all fullness, both physical and spiritual. I was formally baptized by my unbelieving parents as a child. Whether they did that out of tradition or whether someone had persuaded them to do it, I never discovered from their explanations. Now at the age of twenty-six I had decided to renew the grace of baptism.

Like a hardened crust

I knew that the priest himself – the well-known confessor Father Hermogen – would ask me questions and guide my confession. When the day before I read a little booklet in order to prepare myself for confession, I discovered that I had transgressed all the commandments of the Old and New Testaments. But quite independently of that it was clear to me that the whole of my life was full of sins of the most varied kind, of transgressions and unnatural forms of behaviour. They now pursued me and tormented me after my conversion, and lay like a heavy burden on my soul. How could I not have seen earlier how abhorrent and stupid, how boring and sterile sin is? From childhood my eyes had been blindfolded in some way. I longed to make my confession because I already felt with my innermost being that I would receive liberation, that the new person which I had recently discovered within myself would be completely victorious and drive out the old person. For every moment after my conversion I felt inwardly healed and renewed, but at the same time it was as though I was somehow covered with a crust of sin which had grown around me and had become hard. So I too longed for penance, as if for a wash. And I recalled the marvellous words of the Psalm

21

which I had recently learned by heart: 'Purge me with hyssop, and I shall be clean: wash me, and I shall be whiter than snow.'

The experience of a miracle

And so my turn came. I went up, and kissed the gospel and the cross. Of course because I felt dismay and apprehension, I was afraid to say that I was confessing for the first time. Father Hermogen began by asking,

'When did you last fail to go to church? What festivals have you deliberately neglected?'

'All of them,' I replied.

Then Father Hermogen knew that he was dealing with a new convert. In recent times new converts have come into the Russian church in large numbers, and they have to be treated in a different way.

He began by asking about the most terrible, the 'greatest' sins in my life, and I had to tell him my whole biography: a life based on pride and a quest for praise, on arrogant contempt for other people. I told him about my drunkenness and my sexual excesses, my unhappy marriages, the abortions and my inability to love anyone. I also told him about the next period of my life, my preoccupation with yoga and my desire for 'self-fulfilment', for becoming God, without love and without penitence. I spoke for a long time, though I also found it difficult. My shame got in the way and tears took away my breath. At the end I said almost automatically: 'I want to suffer for all my sins, and be purged at least a little from them. Please give me absolution.'

Father Hermogen listened to me attentively, and hardly interrupted. Then he sighed deeply and said, 'Yes, they are grave sins.'

I was given absolution by the grace of God; very easily, it seemed to me: for the space of several years I was to say five times a day the prayer 'Virgin and Mother of God, rejoice', each time with a deep prostration to the ground.

This absolution was a great support to me through all the following years. Our sins (the life of my newly-converted friend was hardly different from my own) somehow seemed to us to be so enormous that we found it hard to believe that they could disappear so simply, with the wave of a priest's hand. But we had already had a miraculous experience: from the nothingness of a meaningless existence bordering on desperation we had come into the Father's house, into the church, which for us was paradise. We knew that with God anything is possible. That helped us to believe that confession did away with sin. And the *starets* also said, 'Don't think about it again. You have confessed and that is enough. If you keep thinking about it you are only sinning all over again.'

My friend's experiences at her first confession were comic in the extreme. She was a young woman called Larissa, a painter and actress, and was making her first confession to a very old monk. The line of those waiting to make their confession was a very long one, and a crowd of old women packed the church, so that many people could hear the confession because of the monk's loud voice. The monk began by putting a question to Larissa which is typical of the kind of penitential conversation that is carried on in Russia nowadays.

'Have you been involved with magic?' was the first question, spoken loudly. In Russia many people practise magic of very different kinds; this is an indication of the lack of Christian education and ignorance of the gospel.

'Yes, I've practised witchcraft,' my friend replied, since she had joined in spiritualist sessions.

'Have you stolen?'

'Yes,' replied Larissa, recalling that as a child she had stolen a jar of marmalade from an aunt.

'Have you killed?' was the monk's third terrifying question.

And Larissa answered in a very low voice, 'Yes.' Abortions are the terrible scourge of the overburdened Russian woman of today.

The old women standing around began to shake their heads, and there were gasps of amazement. Even the old monk was bowled over.

'You should at least be a bit more restrained, my daughter.' This was probably the first time he had been confronted with a new convert, and he did not know who was standing in front of him.

The stones have begun to speak

All that happened ten years ago, when the process first began, a process which today could be described as the Russian religious renaissance. In the course of these years God the Lord sent dozens of pastors to Russia who dared to look after the young people. It is clear that their way was a way of martyrdom from the beginning. The authorities feared nothing more than the newly converted, the new people who entered the church. Educated and full of life, they not only say no to any 'Soviet life-style', but create their own real, beautiful and just world. They change the earth by the power of faith and love.

Today, although it does not have any possibility of 'going out into the world', the Russian church is attracting the best people in Russia, despite its 'muzzled mouth', despite the restrictions and persecutions.

Many Russian priests are rejoicing with all their hearts that 'the stones have begun to speak', that the generations of unbelievers and atheists have now come into the church. But not all can bring themselves to show that they are up with the times, that they can take on themselves the cross of the spiritual and pastoral direction of these young people. Nevertheless, dozens of pastors have devoted themselves to the new converts. They became our loving and wise teachers. In Russia the father confessors and the spiritual fathers were never separated, and the work of the Holy

24

Spirit became particularly evident in the fact that simple, sometimes very young, priests turned into real spiritual leaders and became *startsy*.

What happened to Yevgenii

Our father confessor 'worked' with each of us in different ways; he felt the mystery of each person and God's special plan with him or her. He was a skilful doctor for our souls, even if it took us some years to discover the results of his treatment. I am thinking of what happened to Yevgenii, Yevgenii who was enthusiastic about 'Christian' philosophy, discovering a not very original theory about Christian freedom. It could be summed up in the following words: 'God exists – everything is permissible.' Here Yevgenii referred to some passages in Galatians and the letter of Paul the apostle to the Romans.

His life was fully in accord with his theory: his Don Juan-like tricks increased from day to day. Hurt and abandoned women came to Yevgenii's friends, including me, to complain. They said, 'He believes in God, how can he behave like that?' At the time I thought that Father L., the father confessor whom we shared, perhaps did not know anything about Yevgenii, because Yevgenii often made his confession to him, but never said anything about his adventures and Father L. never asked him about them. One day I asked Father L. directly whether he knew about this dark side of Yevgenii's life. Of course the father confessor knew it all. He said to me: 'Yevgenii is a very sick man. And this sickness lies deeper than his apparently excessive sexual life. We have to work with him for a long time.' Two years passed. Yevgenii is now married and in his letters to me constantly thanks God for the great miracle of love which opened up to him in marriage. He recalls all the 'past' with deep penitence. What happened with Yevgenii is typical. Confession is a high sacrament and a supreme art, and God the Lord sends to his church true doctors, priests, who are brilliant at what they do. Many of our priests who are father confessors are very simple, half-educated 'village priests'. But they see right into people without being deceived, and therefore they are unsurpassed at mastering the most necessary of all arts, the art of discerning the spirits. Indeed the Russian priests recognized the sign of the time and proved up to the tasks laid on them by the church. Some particularly skilful ones emerged, as though they were predestined to hear out the sins of our godless time. These were the ones who succeeded in understanding the new demons of nihilism.

We learned to be ruthless

But the church never took the way of relaxation. I never heard that moral demands in the Russian Orthodox church would be reduced, the moral demands which are only imposed because we live in the century of the 're-evaluation of values', the 'sexual revolution', and so on. For those of us who were new converts it was difficult to accept this new life in all its fullness. We were unaccustomed both to fasts and to regular praying, and even to regular penitential confession. We were not used to accusing ourselves rather than others when anything went wrong. But we gradually learnt that, and in everything we felt the support of God and the church. On the other hand we were very glad that the church preaches the truth which is given once and for all by God, that the commandments of God are not subject to the individual changes that time brings with it. We liked the maximalism of the Christian proclamation: it was only worth living for those things for which people could and would die. We learned to be ruthless about our sins, and we learned to destroy the root of impurity itself. For example it was difficult to describe free relations with someone one loved as 'sexual excesses', which is what they were. We wanted to offer excuses: 'What kind of sin is that? We love each other.' But despite all possible and usual views

26

Christianity calls only for choice and perfection: 'Be perfect, as your Father in heaven is perfect.' And this perfection is something in which not only the soul but also the body is involved. Each of its sighs, each of its movements, is to be dedicated to God.

The high level of demands in Orthodox faith is connected with its extraordinary flexibility and its gentleness towards human beings. How can this contradiction be resolved? Only through love. The specific, wise love which does not seek its like. We find such a love in our pastors, who are endowed with grace to give us freedom. They have freed us from the harsh, oppressive 'karmic' yoke of our past; they have achieved something of which people from non-Christian or pseudo-Christian cultures would not have dreamed. How often has it been written in various philosophies that it is impossible to turn back time, that it is impossible to possess 'what was'. Nietzsche, Heidegger and Proust tormented themselves over this question, and very profound minds and artists still torment themselves over it today.

Their lack of faith makes them slaves of what happened earlier. They do not know that they too are children of God, that a miracle can also happen in their life, that God can also encounter them with his love, as he has encountered all of us.

Father Leonid

Spiritual authority

Since I've been living in the West, it has become clear to me that the crisis of faith here for the most part rests on the fact that there are no true clergy, or almost none; there are no true pastors who can really heal and give good advice and say 'Yes' or 'No' with authority.

What an amazing difference from Russia today! There those who are priests have an amazingly high reputation.

In Russia – both in the cities and in the country areas – there are a great many *batiushki* (literally 'little father', the affectionate designation of a priest) who look after their communities with much love and dedication and see to it that society does not get completely brutalized. And all the people love them deeply: the believers treat their pastor with great respect and when a priest is mentioned one can often hear a word of commendation from atheists, who in any case have long since ceased to be militant.

After the television broadcast in which Father Dmitrii Dudko publicly repented, by chance I happened to hear the conversation of two workers over a glass of beer. 'Did you watch the television yesterday?', one asked the other. 'There's a soft-head! And him a priest!'

The newly-converted intellectuals who had once enjoyed life to the full and had divinized freedom recognize the authority of the priest (I stress, the authority) just as much as the simple man of the people. Many go to the monasteries to make their confession and hear the wise advice of the *startsy*. (*Starets* is an honorary title and means 'the old one'.

Anyone who has the holiness, dignity and wisdom of the old can be given this title.) Even in the nineteenth century the writers Gogol and Dostoevsky, the philosophers Kiriei-evskii and Leontiev went to the monasteries. At that time the monks of the lonely monastery of Optina were particularly well known. But even in the last century the Russian intelligentsia, with few exceptions, were inclined towards positivism and materialism. Today, however, there is a general interest in spiritual questions. Now thousands of young, thoughtful people go to the monks of the small cave monastery of the Transfiguration of Christ near Riga. The monks of the monastery are the best pastors in Russia. And there are also parish clergy who have the gift of freeing people from the power of sin and forming them in a perfect image of God. Not all believers have a pastor, since there are not enough priests. But all Orthodox Christians are concerned to have one. Six years ago we found ours, Father Leonid.

'Come to me after the service'

That came as a great surprise to us, although we had long been looking for a priest to direct us in the spiritual life. When the young people returned to the churches, the clergy were delighted, but they were also afraid of us, for they knew the end of the life of a priest who is surrounded by young people: first, like Father Dmitrii Dudko, he is sent out into the country, further away from the city. But usually this measure doesn't work, since at the weekends hordes of young people fight their way to their pastors; neither the bumpy journey in overfilled buses nor the muddy and impassable village roads have any terror for them. If a priest cannot be restrained by threats, warnings, intrigues and betrayal and continues to remain a true shepherd to his people, one who lays down his life for his friends, then extreme penal measures are adopted, and he is arrested. Long years in prison follow, which also rob his wife and children of the means to exist: they have to drain the cup of suffering to the bitter dregs.

A special grace of God is needed for a priest to be able to decide to go the way of martyrdom. Therefore we were never tempted to condemn their 'fear of suffering', but we understood that we ourselves did not deserve a spiritual father.

Nevertheless, even here God did not abandon us. I remember clearly the evening when we found our pastor. The church was full to bursting. It was so packed that one had the feeling of being squeezed or trampled on. The candles flickered solemnly yet clearly, and more and more of them were produced from the chest for the festival: for St Nicholas, for the Queen of Heaven, for the Saviour, for the Icon of the Mother of God, 'Joy of All the Troubled'.

And despite the disturbances, the crush and the heat, the prayer in the church was unusually urgent: the jubilation and the joy at the wonderful acts of God came from open, honest hearts.

The priest came out and stood in the midst of the faithful, his face turned to the altar. In his glittering, silvery vest-ments he looked like an angel who had come down from heaven to earth.

The faithful then came up to the priest silently to be anointed. In his hand he held a little tassel which he dipped into the holy oil and with it made the sign of the cross on people as they came up. At the same time he quietly said the words, 'In the name of the Father and of the Son and of the Holy Spirit.' When the worshippers kissed him on the hand he added, 'A happy festival!'

His glittering vestments indicated that it was the Feast of the Transfiguration, but it was clear to me that even the rags in which the many unattractive old women were dressed could not destroy the solemn and worthy atmosphere of the festival. Everything was bathed in an unearthly beauty, and nobility and love shone from the young face of the minister.

When I and my two friends went forward to receive the blessing, the priest said to us, 'Come to me after the service.' When we went to him after the service, he suggested that he should become our pastor.

To begin with I was utterly confused. How? Why? What for? What if this was in fact a provocation? Had he been sent for something else as well? How could it be that someone who hardly knew us should make such a serious suggestion? (Father Leonid knew us through his cantor Boris, who earlier had been a poor, insignificant poet.) And above all, how would an ordinary priest with only an average education direct people like us, who led such a complicated intellectual life? All this doubt went through my thoughts like a whirlwind. But urged on by an inexplicable force, the next moment I gave my answer: 'Yes, that would be good.' And my two friends also accepted Father Leonid.

Someone who could give himself completely to another person

That evening in a conversation with him I first understood what a priest really is. There before me I had someone who could give himself not just half-heartedly, but with all his personality and all his soul to another person. There I had met a person who was not just interested in the 'roles' that I was playing in life or even just in my ideas about life, but had a quite personal interest in me, in my particular self which I had always kept hidden because I thought that it would not interest anyone.

We in our intellectual circles had already got used to making critical remarks about books and events, and often also about people. Father Leonid, by contrast, never condemned or even spoke indifferently of anyone. He always spoke of everyone always as though they were his own children, without the sentimentality and blindness which are so typical of physical parents.

31

He was certainly not an intellectual, but with great acumen pointed out to the poets among us the superfluous words, mannerisms or untruths in their poems. I soon came to realize that he could see into people's minds. An apparent triviality or a false overtone were enough for him to draw infallible conclusions to the underlying sickness. He was very patient about healing us. He achieved it quietly, almost without our noticing.

During the Khrushchev era Father Leonid was summoned by the KGB. It was suggested to him that he should give up his priesthood, as many priests had done in that time of cruel and bloody persecutions. They said to him: 'Look, after all only a few old women come to church and soon they too will die out. And then your job will be superfluous anyway.' At that time Father Leonid stood firm. And suddenly, after ten years, young people came back into the church, including intelligentsia, poets, writers, scientists and philosophers. No one would have believed anything like that to be possible.

Father Leonid loved talented people. He wanted poets to be creative again 'to the glory of God' and not bury their talents in the earth. He liked the intelligentsia generally and was as it were made for gradually freeing us from everything that was superfluous, disruptive and sinful. He had to do with people who suffered from megalomania, with 'unrecognized geniuses', with pathologically idle and split personalities, with those who wanted to be loved but were themselves incapable of love. 'To love such an intelligentsia is more difficult than loving one's enemies,' an Italian friend once said to me. An exaggerated view of oneself, an inferiority complex, the lowest dark and neurotic levels of the personality – all that was done away with, the more these people grew into church life and matured in it.

When Father Leonid had heard something important in confession he often stood for a while, lost in thought, with a strained expression on his face. Then he finally said: 'I shall have to pray about that and ask the *matiushka* (the wife of an Orthodox priest) for advice. I'll talk to you next time.' He was never in a hurry to improve someone. Among us new converts there were those who said, 'Father Leonid is too generous: he allows everything.' For of course the young people who had just come to believe in God wanted immediately to change their whole lives radically and finally. Having fallen low, tormented by old sins and wrong-doings, they were athirst to purify themselves through suffering, through hard, genuine penance. Of course there was in this desire that glowing zeal for faith without which Christianity threatens to turn into an indifferent, secularized ideology. But there is also a danger in it, namely an impatient heart, inability for steady and enduring work, excessive tenseness and a tendency to become too easily excited. Moreover there was also an element of the typical Russian character here: like Oblomov, the character created by I.A.Goncharov, the Russian person is ready to die for his beloved idea if only he does not have to spend too long about it!

Creating a perfect icon of God

As a true priest and genuine pastor Father Leonid knew all that, and he acted very carefully, so that at first we often did not even notice. Step by step he then became increasingly demanding and directed his attention to every detail, to every false overtone, to every gesture, every look.

Above all he fought against our arrogance. When, for example, he learned that I had spent a whole evening arguing with two people who were believers but kept away from the church, he said to me, 'Look, you've no right to argue; at most you can give advice. If these people are now put off by the church, it will be your fault.'

He also helped me to put aside false compassion. One of my acquaintances was a lonely, restless, extremely talkative and egocentric woman. She sat at home with me for hours

33

talking until I could hardly bear it any more. But I did not have the courage to interrupt her or once say a hard word to her. I told the *batiushka* about her. His answer was, 'You can cultivate a relationship with anyone you like, but it must not become suicidal. Suicide is sin. Think what the good Samaritan did. He rescued the man, bound up his wounds, found a place for him in the inn and went his way. You must do just the same thing in this case. Help this person as far as you have the strength and go your way. Otherwise her sickness will be stronger than the two of you put together.'

The Holy Spirit certainly works in a person until he or she has reached perfection.

And so each of us was changed in our dealings with this pastor. Those who, for example, used to be terse and tense became more gentle and open; those who used to be talkative pulled themselves together inwardly. People gained a sense of perspective and became beautiful without intending to. That was the aim of all Father Leonid's concerns – to create from our formless chaos a perfect icon of God and to help us to become persons.

First Love

Spiritual hunger

I opened my prayer book in the Metro and began to read the hymn in honour of the Mother of God. A young man was sitting next to me. I noticed how his eyes were glued to the text: he was reading it with me. Opposite us was sitting a young couple. They had deciphered the words *Orthodox Prayer Book* on the cover. Utterly amazed and excited, they looked at each other. When I left the train, the young people also got out and ran up behind me: 'Where can you get that? Please tell us, we would give anything for it.'

All that I could tell them was that I had spent a whole year looking for the prayer book; in Russia, they are even harder to find than the Bible.

In Russia there is spiritual hunger and hunger of the soul. What is the explanation of that? It is more than just a reaction to official atheism, not just an attempt to escape into another world. Nor is it simply to be explained as a search for the meaning of life – that would be too abstract. Nor again is it simply having had enough of ideology, demagogy and general falsehood. For it is something different from disillusionment with secular philosophy. What is happening in Russia today is a phenomenon of a much wider scope, unprecedented and unheard of.

That explains the great rapidity of conversion. Among us, dumb things bring about what even the most brilliant preacher could not achieve in normal circumstances. The first quotation from the gospel found in an atheistic book can change a whole life.

'Repent, for the kingdom of heaven is at hand.' There is probably no place where these words of the Lord have so great a power as in Russia today.

The intelligentsia repent

Conversion and repentance are particularly necessary in fighting against the mother of all sins, pride. It is well known that the intelligentsia have more of a propensity to these vices than any other people. They are particularly enslaved to the idea of their own brilliance and superiority: 'It is hard for a rich man to enter into the kingdom of heaven.' But the intelligentsia have a wealth of riches including some which they are very reluctant to give up: ability, knowledge, talents. Moreover the intelligentsia is poisoned by the cult of a renaissance-like, 'broad' individualism. And it is more difficult for them than for others to go the narrow way of the cross and the truth. And yet all that is taking place. For the first time the Russian intelligentsia is going to church in large numbers, openly and seriously. The intelligentsia is repenting.

It is interesting that this zeal for repentance is so strong in contemporary Russia that sometimes it threatens to turn into nihilistic self-destruction. Many people not only give up their official positions and their career but also turn away from culture altogether, from books and from any attempt to influence the world.

Vladimir I., at one time a capable logician, the pride of the university, wrote that he could no longer carry on with the discipline 'for health reasons'. He gave up his teaching and took one of the lowest paid jobs, becoming a lift attendant. (Half of our seminar work as lift attendants.) But he does not come to our seminar, nor does he go to any other group. He has given away his library to his friends. There are only icons on the walls of his home and he has taken down all his secular paintings. He is at church morning

36

and evening, and the rest of the time it is difficult to see him.

Victor M. is another example. The young man had a brilliant past as an architect and writer, but now he has dropped out. It is said that he has gone with his wife to a distant village where he is working as a verger in the church and thinks back on his pagan past with nothing but horror.

A Christianity without radical claims becomes utilitarian; but there is also another maximalism which can turn into hate for the creation which God made. Often there are believers who have more fear of the devil than love of God. One can find them just as much among simple people as among the newly-converted intellectuals. It has to be said, though, that our *startsy* and father confessors seldom encourage this sharp and radical break with the world. Rather, they summon people not to leave the world but to transform it. As far as possible one is not to give up one's activity but to transform it into the service of God.

A pilgrim came to our church from the Ukraine. She was amazed that there were so many young people here. She was even more amazed when she learned that our parents are all atheists. She burst into tears – she had children who were not believers. She asked us to pray for her children and said, 'Do pray at least once; your prayer goes to God.'

I was directly and immediately convinced of God and could not imagine that people have words, gestures and a language for converse with him. If God the Lord appeared to me through the prayer which he himself spoke, could one still find words which are similar to this prayer? Could they in addition be of such a kind that they could stamp themselves on every soul, speak to our time and solve its problems?

A whole iceberg has to be melted

When Christ preached, to reach the souls of men and women he had to transform the experience of fishermen. To penetrate into the soul of modern people he has to melt a whole iceberg of impressions: he has to overcome history, education, politics, the trivialization of life, the collapse of morality, aestheticism, the revolution – think of all the things that humanity has piled up over these two thousand years! And it is necessary to return to the clear and sublime commandments for blessedness: 'Blessed are the pure in heart, for they shall see God.'

What once seemed incredible is happening in Russia at the moment: both the gospel and the Holy Fathers are emerging at the tip of the iceberg; they are being read again. And it is an extremely modern, extremely intensive and absolutely necessary reading.

Today the time has dawned in Russia in which the truth is being revealed, in all its force, that says of Christ, 'He is the life.'

In fact Soviet people today often describe their ordinary feelings about the world and life like this: 'You go out on the street and everything seems fine: the sun is shining, the birds are singing – but there's no life there.' I was to find the happiest and most cheerful people, those who were most full of joy, in the Russian monasteries. Atheism disappears, as death disappears, when life approaches. I recall a priest, a modest man, living in a village, who had healed a number of people with his prayer. He once told us this story. One day a sick person came to him – apparently fatally ill; he had cancer. Father Vasilii asked him, 'Do you believe in God?' The sick man said, 'No.' Then Father Vasilii asked him, 'Do you want to live?' The sick man replied, 'Yes.' Father Vasilii healed even this sick person, since any thirst for life comes from the Holy Spirit who gives life and fills all things with himself.

It is not as if Soviet life were merely governed by an indifferent atheism. It is guided more by an anonymous inhuman 'fate' which is filled with jealousy. When I carried out an investigation among students, no one said that he or she believed in God. But many said that they would believe in fate. Nowhere in the world do people believe so much in omens: one person adds up the numbers on tram tickets and snaps up the lucky ticket; many are preoccupied with horoscopes; all kinds of gypsies, soothsayers and magicians are popular.

That is also understandable: a tough net has been cast over society, a net of anxiety, of lack of trust in one's own power, of a sense of the impossibility of changing one's life. The experience of total captivity, complete slavery, outside and in, this darkness and harrassment make people take refuge in the last resort in magic. They want to make God gracious once they have enslaved him. But they turn themselves into slaves.

Once many of my friends also lived in this way, with this tremulous belief in fate. Christianity has freed them. Christianity replaces the idea of fate with the idea of the cross. 'For those who are perishing the cross is foolishness, but for us who are saved it is the power of Christ,' says the apostle Paul. Fate enslaves people, stamps them as eternal debtors. People are hesitant to rejoice. But the cross brings freedom in a paradoxical way by putting responsibility on human shoulders. Fate changes people into one thing among other things, a twig which can be bent in any direction. The cross speaks to us of the infinity of divine love and tells us that human beings can even change the divine decision: just as God once spared Nineveh, so too he can spare each one of us. The cross says that prayer can do everything. My conversion took me back to childhood.

The grace of vulnerability

Earlier, like many other people, I lived on greed: greed for knowledge, ability, books and friends. I was always afraid of losing time. But it went devilishly quickly, rushed on like a locomotive gone mad, through the windows of which it was impossible to make out the landscape. Memory did not retain the impressions. At the age of twenty-five I had the feelings of an old woman. I felt as if I had tried and experienced everything. Then came my conversion. It is clear to me that God has affected not only my understanding but also my soul and my heart and all the perceptions of my senses. I feel as I used to in the best moments of childhood. My soul has become pure, innocent and open; it is again capable of being amazed and has thrown off its defences. The world appears to me in a new way, quite directly; it hurts me and it delights me. It is strange, I can no longer remember how I reacted a few months ago in my 'adult' state. It is as though the skin had been sloughed off my soul, as though all protective mechanisms had disappeared with which I once kept my inner life safe from people. Like the rings in trees, walls of ice grew around my real self: irony, self-satisfaction, snobbery, a feeling of indifference. There was a strict hierarchy in terms of which I put people in their place and distinguished between them: there were those who were like me, the élite, and the masses, the herd – all the rest. All that has gone. I became vulnerable. But how good that is! I can breathe freely. Since I discovered God, no day has gone by on which I have felt his absence or his silence. Our father confessor says that this is a divine gift for the newly converted – a flood of grace; that is the way in which one loves very small, helpless children.

The testing of the strong

But I have heard otherwise. Mother Onufria told me that she woke up on the day after taking the habit as a nun, not only without any living sense of the presence of God but also with a coldness in her soul which told her that her whole faith was only deception, that there never had been a God and that there never would be one. After taking the habit Mother Onufria, formerly a woman with a strong and burning faith, felt that she was an atheist. And this state of feeling abandoned by God lasted for several years. God was absent and the whole world around her changed into a dark, gloomy cave. Mother Onufria told the *starets* everything. He explained to her that God sends such testing only to particularly strong children, the most elect and those whom he loves best. The Lord wants people themselves to take the step into the void; he does not want anything to fetter his freedom. And it is clear that the divine grace is a support to our freedom and consequently its limitation. God wants us to love him freely and not for any reason – just as he loves us. God as it were raises up those whom he has chosen into his 'solitude'. And he wants people not just to be slaves, nor even just to be his children, but to be real friends. This sharing in the suffering of being abandoned by God was experienced most powerfully by Jesus Christ himself on Golgotha.

A new perspective

Our life underwent a decisive change because we had acquired a new perspective: our attention shifted from externals to essentials: it moved inside. Whereas earlier we tended to blame society, the KGB or the revolution for all our troubles and our problems, it was now clear to us that we ourselves were guilty of much that contributed to our unhappiness. The endless and barren complaints which are so typical of Russian conversations now came to an end: 'Whose fault is it? What can we do?' A good time began, the time of making a new life. We recognized within ourselves that the Soviet power is not maintained by force of arms, by the KGB, but by anxiety and lies. Its real basis is the

41

mutilated human world. In the tradition of the Holy Fathers our monasteries are called 'saving institutions' and our priests 'doctors': people who have been so seriously ill for such a long time cannot be healed either by ordinary doctors or by the most talented psychologists or psychoanalysts; that can be done only by masters of the 'art', the unselfish fighter for a higher goal, the ascetic: these are people who day by day emerge as victors from the skirmishes of soul and spirit, people who have an art of 'discerning' the spirit which has been lost in the world.

The harvest is ready

Not long ago I was asked to give a lecture on existentialist philosophy in a music school for adults. I did not use any form of pressure on the audience and spoke quite unexpressively. I tried to communicate to them a state of inner tranquillity and prayed in the pauses. There were about forty people in the auditorium, with little intellectual inclination towards the theme: engineers, physicists, workers. Their ages varied between twenty and fifty. My lecture involuntarily turned into a confession: I did not stick to existentialism but went on to Christianity. And that had an unexpected, almost bewildering result: it proved that my lecture had been a spark which had set alight kindling prepared long beforehand. I again recalled Jesus' words, 'The harvest is ready'.

They only let me go towards morning; no one left. Everyone focussed on the most topical questions. It seemed to me that the people sitting in front of me were close to dying of thirst. I had literally to tell them everything: why witnessing to Christ brings joy and is necessary, what a wedding celebrated in church is, and also about the sin of suicide. I began to be ashamed that so many people around me were coming to grief without ever having had the opportunity to receive the gospel. In the last few minutes I answered the question how and where one can be baptized.

Yesterday in our church three girls who were among the audience were baptized. One of them had an important and responsible job in her profession. I told her that her baptism would certainly be reported at her place of work. She just waved her hand and burst out laughing.

My lesson

At confession my father confessor was strict with me for the first time. For the first time he forbade me something. He forbade me to use the word 'I'. I had just come back from the monastery. The few days that I had spent there had been bewildering and unexpected. But that goes without saying: my soul is a vessel which was not prepared to take in so much at a time. When I returned to the city I was like a primed flying bomb. Filled with a stream of energy which had not been there before, I landed on friends and acquaintances with stories about life in the monastery – how I had prayed, how I had read the psalter, how I had hardly eaten or slept. Many of my friends seemed to me to be enthusiastic about what I told them. They wanted to go to this monastery straightaway in order to find the 'Holy Spirit'. Only my father confessor, usually generous, reacted in an unusual way. He noted the arrogance in my enthusiasm, and he forbade me to use the word 'I'.

At the time I could hardly understand. But then God showed me some women as examples. And I recognized that real beauty is silent and says virtually nothing.

One sometimes comes across amazing faces in church, faces in which there is not a superfluous line, in which there is nothing physical. They are faces like icons, faces from which the pure flame of prayer has burnt away all passion, all vanity and all heaviness. A woman stands in our church, almost in the remotest corner, not striking in any way. She never speaks to anyone, is the first to come to church and the last to go. Her eyes shine in her gentle and happy face. It is of such inconceivable and at the same time such hidden

43

beauty that one involuntarily thinks of the parable of the treasure hidden in the field, for which a person gives away everything else. For a long time I had wanted to talk to her. I went up to her awkwardly and clumsily said to her, 'Do you stand here every day like that?'

A very bright smile crept over her face: 'I'm not sure.'

I learned my lesson: don't rush around everywhere out of curiosity; don't be curious; forget yourself.

More than a sense of one's own worth

Guilt feelings are very strong among the newly converted. They are tormented by their past, in which their lives were worse than that of any criminal, because they wanted to try out and experience everything for themselves – there was no teacher! The feeling of guilt is a new, sublime feeling. It is not to be confused with the Soviet, Kafkaesque complex of universal guilt and damnation.

For us, conversion to Christianity is normally accompanied by a phase of fighting against false guilt, by anxiety and mistrust. All that is the result of utter totalitarianism. Perfect totalitarianism does not need anyone with honest convictions. On the contrary, totalitarianism eliminates these before it is finally established. Totalitarianism celebrates its triumph when everyone lies, from top to bottom. The general tendency to lie, involvement in something immoral and false, also creates the illusion of strength. It seems as if power is eternal and unshakable, The people are sunk in hopelessness. The oppressive atmosphere of hopelessness dominates the population without any limits. In this spiritual vacuum the most important thing to begin with is to find a sense of one's own worth, the 'complex of respectability', what Solzhenitsyn called 'No longer living with a lie.'

Therefore the dissidents have also begun the struggle for human rights. The opposition have made it their task to oppose the decline of the people into hopelessness, to

44

arouse the will to fight. So today in Russia the fighters for human rights are seeking, even with their blood, to overcome anxiety and to restore to people faith in their own capabilities.

The dissidents have begun by freeing personality. The new Christians have to go one stage further. Now that they have overcome their anxiety and despair they no longer shape their life according to the principle of resistance. They discover other values, positive and creative. In heroism they recognized not only good but also dangerous features – love of self, theatricalism, egocentric self-confidence. They also discovered the weakness in heroism, and saw the danger that fearlessness might be diverted into a self-satisfied and superficial Soviet humanism. In Soviet schools we were all stuffed full of Gorki's words: 'Man – that's a proud word'.

What was the strength and stay of atheism became a hindrance in Christianity. The newly converted put the fear of God higher than self-concern and fearlessness; the feeling of human self-regard paled in the light of the beautiful and liberating feeling of guilt: about all people and all things. The feeling of guilt grew stronger and the feeling of responsibility for all those who suffer and are oppressed grew deeper. In the Russian monasteries we found a universalism which met the needs of our hearts. There people prayed for the whole world, and in the late evening prayer this intention is sometimes indeed made quite precise: 'And now let us pray, brothers and sisters, for those who cannot pray themselves, and also for those who have no one to pray for them. Let us pray to the mother of God. "Under your protection…"'

Everything in the church was new

There is still too much philosophy in Russia today. It's as it was in the nineteenth century: the Russian intelligentsia is engaged in reading everything that comes to us from the West. An enormous number of translations are in circulation

45

in the underground literature. There are arguments all night long in Moscow and Leningrad kitchens about Jaspers and Husserl, Sartre and Lévi-Strauss. I remember how my friends and I often discussed the problem of time, agreeing with the ideas of Bergson and Heidegger, that rationalist philosophy can only describe the past. The understanding and reason, by nature demonstrative and serving to make things tangible, have a relationship to what has come into being, what is complete, what already was. We liked Heidegger's study of Nietzsche, in which he derived rationalism from voluntarism. From Leibniz to Schopenhauer and Nietzsche the philosophy of rationalism and the Enlightenment was a philosophy of the will. In his work Heidegger deciphered Nietzsche's favourite idea, the idea of the 'eternal return'. The will can do everything but bring back the past. Therefore the will takes its revenge on time and invents the idea of the eternal return of the one and the same. But reason is also founded on this law of the eternal return to the past.

We were equally children of Russia and Europe; we felt hemmed in by the framework of voluntaristic and rationalistic culture, where the past hangs over the present, where one cannot improve anything, where Sisyphus will endlessly roll his stone up the hill and humanity is enslaved for all time by the corruptness of our actions, mistakes and follies. Now when I recall this feeling I can say that we lived in a hell. For one of the characteristics of boredom in hell is uniform monotony.

And then something else suddenly dawned. The perspective of forgiveness and atonement, unexpected earlier, was suddenly bathed in full light. Christianity freed us from the oppressive karma of the past. Repentance and the confession of sins made possible what was impossible before. The past disappeared, it was no longer there.

The church conquered what seemed unconquerable.

The satiation of eternal recurrence was countered with

46

that unique historical event of the resurrection. In the church everything was new: both then, when as it were in ignorance we went into it for the first time, but also four or five years later. The eucharist is always unique and unrepeatable. Love for the church is always first love.

Our Seminar

The beginning

At one stage the well-known Leningrad poet Sergei Stratonovskii came to me. Sergei was one of those Russian intellectuals of whom Dostoevsky once said, 'They do not need a million. One has only to let them think.' Sergei is an agnostic. I had no objections to that. By the beginning of the 1970s everyone in our circles was already a believer. Some had come to Christ after very complicated psychological and spiritual quests. Some had come too simply, because in our circles not to be a believer was already regarded as provincial and retrogressive. Being a Christian and being cultivated were thought to amount to virtually the same thing. In such circumstances it is not easy to remain an atheist or even an agnostic. Sergei was too honest and inwardly also too self-critical to speak from the position of faith, like everyone else. He remained a sceptic.

What concerned him deeply and seriously was a cultural problem. He could not understand how religion had always been the beginning of European culture and its breeding ground, so that the word 'culture' is itself derived from the word 'cult'. Sergei proposed that we should form a seminar in the philosophy of religion in which the church fathers and contemporary theologians would be studied. The first meetings of our seminar took place in 1973.

In basement apartment no. 37

We always met in different buildings.

The seminar became particularly popular when we began

to meet in the damp but roomy basement apartment no. 37. Every Friday dozens and sometimes hundreds of people came to this place. They sat on the floor because of course there were far from enough chairs. They spread out into all the rooms and listened to the lectures with increasing silence. We began with the simplest things, with what was to form a general basis. At that time the Public Library in Leningrad was not yet closed to us, as it is today to most of the 'unofficial intellectuals'. At that time, too, editions of church authors which had appeared before the Revolution had not yet been taken off the shelves. So we read the texts of Gregory the Theologian, Basil the Great, Origen, Athanasius the Great and Tertullian. We fell on them with great enthusiasm, as on no other literature. The archaic character of the language did not hold us back, nor could the fact that their problems and disputes lay long in the past damp our ardour. These authors were close to us, we had as it were found only what we knew, but it was infinitely more sublime and spiritually more mature than we were ourselves. Here we were addressed by an unassailable church authority.

Those who came to our seminar

What sort of people came to our seminar? People met there from different social strata and very different backgrounds. There were artists and poets who did not belong to the official cultural circles; there were philosophers who did simple work somewhere to earn a living and who produced their books on underground presses. There were physicists, mathematicians who were investigating the deeper meaning of things. There were pupils from the senior grades and old people who had still known the religious circles of the period after the Revolution, circles which had been destroyed in the 1930s. There were scientists who had achieved a worldwide reputation through their books. And there were the special cases without which Russia would not be what it is: evidently crazy people, in touch with other worlds and extra-terrestrial beings. Even an 'illegal' Marxist came: illegal because he had discovered the 'authentic' Marx and from this standpoint criticized our society as a society of 'state capitalism'. His rare but energetic objections usually cheered everyone up, since none of us took Marxism seriously any longer. It was particularly comic to hear him repeating, with the strict face of a fanatic sectarian, 'religion is the opium of the people'.

But in the main we had the creative intelligence of people between twenty-five and forty, people in search of innovation, indeed thirsting for it. The nucleus of the seminar was made up of five or six new Orthodox converts. They always took part in the sessions and also gave papers. Each of them had made his or her own way to God. When I saw their purified, joyful faces I could hardly believe that things had once been completely different.

Some biographies of believers

There was the life of Sasha P., who nowadays cannot be parted from the letters of Paul and knows them almost off by heart. Every day he gathers young people around him to read the letters aloud to them and to discuss with them. I've known Sasha for more than ten years. He is now twenty-eight. At school he was first in the class, the best mathematician, a well-known poet. At the age of twenty he became enthusiastic about Nietzsche and Freud. At twenty-three he began to drink, let himself go, lost interest and quickly went under. Not only I but many of us recalled how he would regularly stand at one of the tables in the cafe, silent and staring vacantly into space. Then he got into a psychiatric hospital, where for the first time in his life he came to know Christians. He began his way into a new life. When he was released from hospital he immediately went to church, had himself baptized and felt reborn. Many of my acquaintances have had this experience on being

50

baptized at a mature age: they tangibly experienced in themselves the whole power of this mystery which made their faith firm and unshakable.

Here is a second biography: the story of a wise, courageous and talented woman, Galina G. After leaving school she developed the view that really free and creative people live outside social structures and roles. She broke off connections with her 'bourgeois' background character and went into the artistic underground. The usual artists' life began: writing verses at night, unofficial readings, endless sessions with the usual empty intellectual discussions. Freedom in everything: in love, in exchanges of tendencies and authorities, in a hysterical and chaotic existence. Then the attempt to end her life by suicide, an attempt which luckily failed. By chance she met some people who practised yoga. After that her life changed quickly. Galina stopped drinking, ate only fruit and vegetables and looked down her nose at the dirty world around her. As a practitioner of yoga she went into a Christian church to feel the divine 'energies'. (Those who practise yoga often told me that they could meditate best in a church.) Then she began to accept Christian faith. She was convinced that the sign of the cross, like any mantra, was the true way to the absolute and to self-realization. Finally she began to sing in the choir with the old ladies, and after she had given up her 'om om', to say the words of the most profound Christian prayers. In the course of a few weeks she 'felt' Christianity as a religion with quite a different spirit from Hinduism. She understood that Christianity was closer to her, that it bestowed a particular power and blessing on her, that she was freed through it. After that she called yoga 'kindergarten'.

Another example is Slava D. In the past he was a Soviet sociologist with a successful career, taking part in numerous sociological congresses, even at an international level. Like most people in that sphere he led a split life: at party meetings he gave speeches and called for implementation of the resolutions of the last Party Day. But in the evening, among friends, he would tell anti-Soviet anecdotes. At some point his conscience became aroused and he began to understand that this was no life for him. After the invasion of Czechoslovakia in 1968 he gave in his party card. That meant that he lost his work, his former friends, everything that had so far made his life meaningful. He was filled with a cold hatred for everyone, for this régime, for this country, for these enslaved people around us. His wife, a quiet and shy person, brought him to Christianity. At a later stage he confessed to me, 'I can see how beautiful people's faces are when they pray.' Now he is studying Origen, and he has been asked to give the main lectures on this theologian at the seminar.

I could add a dozen such biographies, and each of them would be unique. If one reflects on all these destinies, one can understand that in itself faith was not just a transitory ideological enthusiasm. In fact conversion not only affected people's spiritual and intellectual convictions but also changed their views of themselves and the world. The change was permanent and complete, and embraced body and Spirit. Christianity created these people anew. They learned to see with new eyes; their voices became deep and tranquil; and the restlessness and nervousness disappeared from their faces. Their whole beings radiated naturalness and harmony.

The main lecturers and the most important members of the seminar were Orthodox Christians. But as well as them there were also Catholics and the agnostics. The Catholics had formed a small ecumenical seminar in Leningrad: some of us went to it on Wednesdays to pray the rosary. From our Catholic friends we learned for the first time of the appearance of the Mother of God at Fatima and what she had said there about Russia. That not only made us glad, but also gave us a feeling of enormous responsibility: the fate of the whole world depends on the fate of Christianity in Russia.

Our relations with the Baptists

One day the Leningrad '*iniziativniki* Baptists' (i.e. the unofficial Baptists) learned of our existence. These were people who despite the prohibition continued to instruct their children in the Christian faith without having their congregations registered. They deliberately and unshakably chose the way of martyrdom for themselves. These Baptists usually listened to all the lectures, all our chaotic discussions which could last for hours. Clearly there was much that they did not understand, and other things lay outside their experience and their problems. As these were very simple people, they were not interested in specific cultural questions. (In the first years of its existence Soviet power exterminated the educated Protestants.) But they regarded us as people who believed honestly and passionately. That brought us closer together, regardless of all other differences. When our discussions eventually became more peaceful, one of the Baptist preachers would regularly get up, open the Bible and speak. His sermons did not have particularly elegant phrases or arguments, had no unexpected dialectic and certainly no philosophical depth. These were simple words about simple things. But they were delivered with such power and conviction, with such readiness to stand by every word before the invisible Judge that we could not avoid being moved by them and recalling the word of the gospel: 'And the Lord has chosen the foolish things of the world to shame the wise, and the insignificant things to shame the significant.'

Of course our relations with the Baptists were not always so harmonious. There were also differences between us, and we had passionate arguments with one another. One day we planned to discuss the theme of Christian marriage. It was clear that for many Orthodox who in their earlier

53

pagan phase had experienced both the sexual revolution and more than one divorce, the way of monasticism was particularly attractive alongside the ideal of Christian marriage. Becoming a monk was one way of atoning for all the sins of a burdensome past. Many people already lived like monks in the world (we could not get into a monastery). They longed so much to make up for past wrongdoings, and felt such pressure to give up everything and take the hardest way. However, for the Baptists, who consistently put forward Luther's viewpoint, monasticism was not an option. They did not recognize its existence. Indeed, they regarded our journeys to the *startsy* as great sins, as they did our love for the icons, the fast days, and our tendency towards asceticism. Even when they began to speak about this openly and argued from scripture that the icon was an idol, a pagan image, their listeners still kept quiet. They knew that the Protestants had their peculiarities. But when one of their preachers got more and more agitated and began to say something against the Mother of God, a storm of unrest burst out which threatened to turn into a real religious war. At that time I was in the chair at the seminar and did not know how to settle the dispute. The Baptists left us in anger, feeling deeply alienated.

Later, after some time had passed and we began to feel ashamed, we invited our Protestant friends back again, though of course not those from whom we could expect barren and bad-tempered disputes.

Atheists also came

There were not only believers in the seminar, but atheists also came, people who ought more really to be termed sceptics or agnostics. They were interested in religion as a sphere in which the human spirit shows itself with extreme profundity and great seriousness. Some recognized that the Gospels are the most brilliant books in the history of humanity. Others respected Jesus as a human being. A

54

third group believed in the philosophical Absolute and a fourth in some kind of mystery; the fifth simply wanted to be up-to-date with the modern spiritual quest. After the seminar had been in existence for a few years, many of the waverers believed in the personal God, the Holy Trinity and the apostolic church.

We prized mutual freedom too much to force our religious convictions on others. At the same time those who believed had the feeling that time was on our side. And this feeling was supported by everyday experience. My philosophical friends had recently grieved over me and mocked me: 'She's gone off to the old women who can neither read nor write; she's lost to philosophy.' Barely two years had gone by before they had all themselves accepted Christian faith, one at the age of thirty and another at the age of thirty-five. And I was their godmother.

The informers were also there

From the beginning the founding and work of the seminar seemed a tremendous venture, and doomed to disaster. No one believed that we could exist for long. Rumours regularly spread through the city that the organizers of the seminar had already been arrested. Of course we welcomed anyone without exception into the house. Nor did we make any attempt at a conspiracy. Given the conditions prevailing in Russia it is impossible to hide oneself from the all-seeing eye of the KGB, quite apart from the fact that it would have been dangerous to 'play' at being illegals. That would have drawn down even more suspicion on us. In the course of the whole of the ten years the KGB limited itself to very 'gentle' measures: there were always informers in our seminars. From the 'conversations' with the KGB it became clear to me that the secret service was well informed about what had been said in the seminar. In the official Soviet journal *Ogoniok* an article appeared exposing the seminar. People often picked me up off the street and took me for a conversation with the KGB, where different methods and threats were used to try to dissuade me from organizing any more of these gatherings. Some students were expelled from institutes, others who took part in our meetings lost their jobs, rumours were spread, gossip went the rounds, to bring us down. But the seminar in Leningrad still exists today.

We were more worried by the anxieties and psychoses of our Leningrad intellectuals than by the KGB. For a long time some of them could not get used to the idea that we existed freely. Doubts began: is the seminar perhaps a provocation? Has the KGB perhaps organized it with the purpose of detecting all Christians and free-thinkers and keeping them under constant control? These conversations gradually stopped. People got used to the fact that no one was shot or put in prison. The fearful relaxed. There were even jokes: it was said that on Fridays you could tell anti-Soviet jokes in any house without danger since all the informers were in No.37.

Like the prodigal son

For two years the work of the seminar was predominantly devoted to the study of the church fathers. In addition we read and discussed on topics connected with modern theology. By chance a German tourist had brought us some books by Karl Rahner and Hans Urs von Balthasar. Among the Protestant theologians, similarly by chance, we came across the works of Karl Barth and Paul Tillich. Many people loved Kierkegaard and some knew him almost off by heart, but of course only as a writer, and not as an important church thinker. We devoted some discussion to Russian philosophy of religion: Fr Pavel Florenskii, Father Sergei Bulgakov, Berdyaev, Rozanov. Among us there were pupils both of Florenskii and of Berdyaev and Rozanov. Of course these last were writers of fifty years ago. Since that time the whole of Russian life has changed radically. Russia has gone through the purifying fire of suffering. Here God was almost killed, and after God, millions of completely innocent people were murdered. Culture, historical consciousness and what one might call national memory were completely or almost completely exterminated.

Right at the beginning of this century the Russian intelligentsia began to have their eyes opened. Its best representatives moved on from Marxism to Idealism and from Idealism to Christian realism. From the beginning of the century this brought the intelligentsia, like the prodigal son, back to the church. Associations for the philosophy of religion were organized in which on the one hand the voice of the particularly progressive and open representatives of the hierarchy could be heard and on the other hand writers, philosophers and journalists. If one reads the minutes of those gatherings they seem to have been written in a completely different age. The intelligentsia, who had newly discovered for themselves the deep and mysterious meaning of Christian faith, could not at that stage be content with the passiveness, the immobility and the conservatism of the Orthodox church. Vast numbers of reforms and innovations were proposed to 'renew' the old fabric of the church! If we look at our own time we find the church even more passive – indeed one might say that it was completely suppressed by the state. But none of us has ever accused our church, criticized it from outside or called for innovations. And if that should really come about, it would only be in the first flush of conversion, when the person concerned had yet to discover the whole fullness of church life, and it will have taken place for convenience. For it is difficult and strange to enter into a completely different rhythm of life, to read morning and evening prayers, to stand all the way through a three-hour liturgy. Today the Russian intelligentsia are sufficiently 'poor' to look for the reason for the evil that exists not in some other place but in oneself, in order to arrive at the essential point at which the

57

transformation of one's whole life begins: repentance. 'Do not live with the feeling of illness, but with the feeling of guilt,' says Berdyaev. The understanding of the church itself became different: deeper and more mystical. In the totalitarian state the church presented itself to us as the only pure and really living island in life. It became the antithesis of any ideology that kills and stifles. And in our state the power of ideology is in fact total. Ideology corrupts the personality, but in the church a person can grow to complete fullness. Ideology lives as a parasite on the feelings, on human unhappiness. In the church human beings communicate truly and creatively, in a communication without lies. Either the human body or the human spirit is always oppressed by ideology; in the church such a dualism is overcome. Here we find a fullness of spirit and body. We do not now understand the church as a state institution but as the body of Christ, as a new life directed towards the resurrection of the whole creation.

There are only two possibilities

The Leningrad seminar concentrated on the problems of Christian culture and anthropology. We have seen that in the twentieth century one can no longer talk of human beings as people did in the seventeenth and eighteenth centuries, that the experience of the annihilation at Hiroshima, in Auschwitz, and in the Gulag inevitably changes our idea of humanism substantially. Now we cannot irrefutably derive human beings from or reduce them to a class analysis or a biological substance or to what is 'human, all too human'. The human being is the 'sphere of openness', the 'cleft in Being-there' (Martin Heidegger). The human being is 'being on the boundary' (Karl Jaspers). We did not just appropriate the anthropological echatologism of the existentialists in theory – it went into our flesh and blood. We lived constantly and daily on the boundary. After we had become Christians we continued to develop the echatologism of modern thought. The 'new man', the 'new creation' of whom we now spoke, was not open for just any possibility. He was open for radical decision. His responsibility included a choice between God and the devil, between decline and deliverance. Our thought was maximalist: spiritual values or materialism, the way of contentment or the way of Christ. There was no third possibility. For us, both culture and daily life were a living and creative commentary on the eternal truths of the church tradition. Eternity was no longer a poetic invention or a 'bath with spiders' (to use the description given by Svidrigailov, a figure from Dostoevsky's *Crime and Punishment*). It was a reality which increasingly seized us and did so in a vigorous way. 'Behold, I make all things new': the Holy Spirit showed himself by putting all possible modern spiritual tendencies and ideologies in the shade by the light of his innovation.

In later years the meetings of our seminar always took place on Sundays. We met in our church for worship, made our confessions, received the eucharist and then went to someone's home. We soon stopped having a fixed place but changed the place where we met, so as not to expose those who lived there to any danger. In matters like this KGB thinking runs along stereotyped materialist lines: A seminar? Where? Who owns the building? The person living there could lose his job, could be refused permission to live in Leningrad. In a state which is involved in everything and covers everything there are many ways of ruining a person's life.

The Moscow seminar

The Leningrad seminar had already been in existence for some years when we learned that in Moscow intellectuals had similar seminar meetings. The names of Alexander Ogorodnikov, Vladimir Poresh, Tatiana Shchtipkova stood out. We kept hearing rumours of serious persecutions of the Moscow seminar. Regelson, a member of the Committee

'For the Protection of Believers', was arrested. When these arrests began it soon became clear to us that we could not keep silent. We wrote and published some letters in defence of the Moscow seminar and tried to make contact with those who had not yet been arrested.

The seminar in Moscow, like our own, had been founded by new converts. Moscow and Leningrad have always been different: Moscow is dominated by a more earthy, more Russian spirit. Petersburg/Leningrad has always been a city directed towards Europe which was built on nothing, on marshy land. Dostoevsky called it 'the most ingenious city in the world'. Whereas our Leningrad seminar was very varied in composition – Nietzscheans and those who practised Yoga, Muslims and Orthodox monks came along – in Moscow a more 'mature', only Orthodox, public met. There was a good deal of discussion there about the future and the predestined role of Russia. Before the beginning of the seminar they prayed for the Russian martyrs, and mentioned aloud the names of the bishops, priests and laity who were tortured to death by the Bolsheviks. All that formed the themes and conversations of the new Russia. In it there was no trace of conservatism, no wish for restoration or a return to the old pre-revolutionary way of things. The Orthodox faith had opened the eyes of many people to the fact that they have a homeland which is new and eternal. One hears nothing of it in the Soviet papers, but it exists, it is reborn from the ashes: the Russia of St Boris and St Gleb, St Sergei Radoneshskii and St Seraphim Sarovskii. More than its greater interest in specifically Russian themes distinguished the Moscow seminar from the Leningrad seminar. Our Moscow friends were also concerned to realize in practice the ideal of an authentic community life. As is well known, in the Soviet Union the church cannot have a congregational life. Therefore the attempt to establish an authentic living community was an enormous threat to the existing social structure which was marked by its inhumanity and cruelty. But that is precisely where the power of the new Christians lies in Russia today: they do not fight with the existing system, they do not unmask its corrupt and unscrupulous leaders, but positively build up a new reality, once they have found inner freedom. By the example of their whole lives they create the true and future church. They already live in a new way and therefore are already victorious.

All the members of the Moscow seminar have now been arrested. Those who took part in it paid a high price for their freedom. It seems to me that one of the reasons why the Leningrad seminar still meets and the Moscow seminar does not lies in the social and political orientation of the Moscow seminar, namely in the attempt of its participants to be Christians in a very specific and therefore dangerous sense of the word, by seeking to form a Christian community.

Lord, help your servants Alexander, Vladimir, Tatiana, Victor, Sergei, Gleb; do not abandon those who follow you on the way to the cross!

He has no Form or Comeliness

On the road in a Soviet suburb

We were on the long road from the suburban line to the house of brother Volodya. It was a raw and cold Petersburg autumn, and our feet sank into the mud; we were looked down on by the grey, featureless and cold fronts of the standard, four-storey houses which are quite indistinguishable from one another and form the anonymous and mute world of new Soviet building developments. Perhaps a new Kafka will describe them. But against this background both the Kafkaesque state of damnation and the hopeless situation that he depicts will prove to be a special literary experience. This architecture is itself simply a reflection of the omnipotent power of the Great Inquisitor who has freed human beings from God, from tradition and from themselves.

Everything seemed to indicate that the people with whom I was now going to the first Baptist meeting of my life must inevitably be in the grips of the same anonymous power of the Grand Inquisitor. Unlike my friends, they did not belong to the confused and sceptical intelligentsia. Like all 'normal' Soviet people, from childhood on they lived as it were behind the looking glass, in our Soviet dark, where lies are obligatory, mistrust is unavoidable and anxiety is everywhere. It seemed to me that I was dealing with 'simple people', although I already knew that one of them had spent twenty-five years in the gulag.

Finally we had left this new Soviet building development behind us and came to the end of this suburb, where there were still a few wooden peasant huts. We went into one of them; it was roomy and full of wooden seats.

My first Baptist meeting

At the front there was a table, and on the table was a linen cloth on which there was written, in large letters, 'God is love'. It all seemed strange, bleak and out of place to an Orthodox Christian like myself. Almost automatically I compared it unfavourably with a room for party meetings. I was accustomed to the majestic, mysterious and mystical beauty of the Orthodox churches. I had come to take it for granted that the temple of God is heaven on earth.

About forty people came, all the same 'ordinary', average people. Certainly what stood out was their inner composure, their quiet solemnity, their restraint, coupled at the same time with openness. What struck me were the unusual gestures that these people cultivated: their special way of walking, their gaze – something that is not achieved by worldly training, but appears only as the reflection of a deep, inner seriousness.

The meeting began with a prayer, which was read out by the oldest of the preachers, a fragile old man with grey hair. Then all present began to kneel down spontaneously and to pray. And there I discovered an amazing thing: I was listening to a confession of guilt which, as in the early church, was said out loud, before the people, in the presence of all.

Unless you become like children

What happened then completely surprised me; it again wiped away illusion and malicious thoughts. Children spoke next. They recited the Gospels page by page, off by heart; they were serious and wise. Up to this point I had believed that the purity of children is an adult myth, and I shared the view of Freud, who had said that the child is 'perverted in many ways'. I recalled how deceptive I myself had been as a child, how I had been able to play different roles to my advantage. The children of my intellectual acquaintances, who were always wanting to be the centre of attention, increased my unwillingness. And suddenly I saw right in front of me an illustration of the gospel: 'Unless you are converted and become like children you will not enter the kingdom of heaven.'

Later I saw small children in Orthodox monasteries not more than six or seven years old, who would stand still right through long liturgies. They really prayed, and knew what conversation with God means.

In the earnestness of these children who recited holy scripture off by heart, I in fact felt that there was something there, something that was more than a game. Later I met children making their confession and even martyr children. Even in school they were hurtling towards what was later to be their daily fate. In school the teachers mocked children who were believers and encouraged their classmates to torment them. But these children bravely bore the torments – and indeed the blows. They already deliberately went the way of the cross, so powerfully did the living God speak in their souls.

Monks from Athos who have spent some time in Russian monasteries told me that these Russian children will judge them in the next world.

Those whose hearts are full have to speak

After the Bible reading they sang some extremely simple and primitive verses, of no aesthetic merit, to the accompaniment of guitars. At another time I would have called them kitsch. The music was not much better than the verses, and the tunes were taken from current Soviet songs. But the honesty won. The voices trembled as if they were speaking the name of God for the first time. Then came the sermon. It was given by a man of about fifty. He held a Bible in his hands. The most interesting part of his address was the testimony about his life. He himself was a Finn; he had married a Russian girl twenty years earlier and had settled in Leningrad. In Finland he had belonged to the Lutheran tradition. When he got to Leningrad he began to seek out his brothers in the faith. He was told that there was the Baptist church. There were two, one which was allowed, and another which was banned and persecuted. Then he was asked which one he wanted to join: 'The persecuted one, of course,' he said. So he joined the unofficial Baptists, the *'iniziativniki'*.

Over the course of the years he was arrested four times. A KGB officer once asked him, 'What right do you have to speak of God without permission? Show me your permit.' Then Brother N. opened the gospel and read out, 'Those whose hearts are full have to speak.' 'That's my permission,' he said.

After Brother N. a young man in sailor's uniform came forward and said that faith had changed his whole life. Earlier he had been a drunkard, thought only of money, and was slowly turning into an animal.

All the rest listened to him attentively and silently. Only one of those present behaved in a strange way; he wept and sighed, beat his breast continually and said aloud, 'I, too, Lord, was a drunkard, a liar and a thief. I have constantly betrayed you, Lord.'

After the meeting I asked a brother why this man express-ed his feelings so openly. I was told that he was a member of the Pentecostal community and that while the Baptists are marked by self-control and inner composure, another element is dominant among the Pentecostalists. There people are not afraid to be emotional and even have ceremonies with dances and songs; often they speak with tongues, and have revelations and healings.

65

'He had neither form nor comeliness...'

The last address was given by a brother who had come from the Ukraine. On the way to this suburb of Leningrad he had stopped at many places where there were Baptist communities. Everywhere he preached to his brothers. He told us how they had killed his younger brother Pyotr in the army. Pyotr had refused to pick up a rifle, so he was beaten to death.

This preacher from the Ukraine was a completely uneducated man. He stressed words wrongly and always spoke in a halting way. Sometimes he even adopted an exaggerated and solemn tone which gave unnatural strength to his voice.

I was involuntarily reminded (by my wicked and ironical memory) that in our philosophy faculty, where Komsomols and party speakers learned and taught with us, the conviction arose that the main thing for such people was to learn to speak loudly and with self-confidence, and even shout where necessary. But even the outward similarity with an official Soviet party speaker could not conceal from us, the congregation, the power and truth of what the brother was saying. Despite the strange form of the expressions, which somehow did not seem right, the voice of a confessor came through, a voice in which there was neither self-confidence nor even confidence, but faith. And for yet another time in the course of the evening the words of the prophet Isaiah went through my head: 'He had neither form nor comeliness that we could look on him. He did not look such that we could have pleasure in him. He was despised and rejected, a man of sorrows and acquainted with grief; as one before whom one covers the face he was despised...'

The Holy Spirit despises no one

Then again there followed a time of general prayer. A woman regretted that she could not help her husband, an unbeliever and a drunkard, and was incapable of saving him and showing him the world that she had found. Another spoke of her headaches and her illnesses and thanked God for them. This woman looked like a housewife and a cook; she seemed the sort that usually attracted my attention when they were secretly observing their neighbours in the block, shouting in shops and chattering in queues. And suddenly – she spoke so profoundly, words which went to the heart like a psalm, and so honestly, out of deep grief and strength of spirit. There was joy and ease in her words when she thanked God. She knew that she should not just forget her everyday life with its thousands of petty cares. Rather, she changed the heaviness and monotony of life, its toughness and ugliness, into a reality illuminated and given by God. Earlier I had despised her and her like and thought that they had gone crazy at their kitchen sinks: I did not think that they were human. But now I am ashamed. I gladly confess that. It is clear that the Christian can serve God anywhere. As St Simeon the New Theologian said, 'The Holy Spirit is not afraid of anything and despises no one.'

A Day in the Monastery

Only a few monasteries are left in modern Russia. There are about twelve, which are almost all in the republics which were incorporated after the war: in Esthonia, Latvia, Lithuania and the Ukraine. There they were not closed, so they came to us as a cultural and spiritual heritage.

We went to the monastery for a week. A longer stay was impossible. The time is stipulated in the pass for the monastery. But three days in the monastery were enough for us to shake off our worldly powerlessness, to be able to breathe to the full the spiritual atmosphere that we needed to be able to go out boldly with new strength to fight again in the world.

Here are my impressions of a monastery. They do not deal with what I feel to be the most important thing: the mysterious and deep world of worship and prayer in the monastery. Here I only want to talk about people that we – my girl friend and I – met in the monastery, from that time when we got on the bus one day in Pskov to go to Pechory, the village in which the monastery is situated.

Father Alexander

First of all there was Father Alexander. He sat opposite us in the stuffy and jolting bus, a typical village priest. Of course he was not wearing the soutane: that is strictly forbidden. We recognized him by certain old-fashioned features: the blue-black old cloak, a round grey hat, the thin beard, the suitcase on his lap. Father Alexander began to speak to us loudly with great enthusiasm. All the travellers listened to him, some nodding in agreement and paying attention, and others with quiet laughter. Yet others were offended or quite obviously angry. He talked for the whole journey – an hour and a half.

Father Alexander served in some remote village. He was an outstanding, talented preacher. He had often been the bane of atheistic officials.

'And I want to tell you another thing, Comrade Aloginov – the family name of one of his opponents – I am not a relic of capitalism but a relic of Communism. I first saw the light of the world under Soviet power. I served in the fleet for seven years and fought with the partisans; I've worked in a factory and I found God after a great deal of experience and a great deal of reflection.'

'And as for the perfection of matter, I can tell you, Comrade Aloginov, that life has never simply turned out well; it has always been full of sharp contradictions and tragedies.'

'They write, Comrade Aloginov, that all Soviet people are marching forwards and following the most progressive ideology in the world. But I tell you that a hundred per cent of the men in my parish are not behind the most progressive view of the world but behind the vodka bottle.'

Father Alexander told how he had often been questioned by the police because of his 'religious propaganda'.

The police asked him, 'Is it true that you have said that there is no freedom among us?'

Father Alexander replied, 'For me there is freedom only in Christ. As for any other freedom, all I can say is that if it existed, I would not be sitting here.'

People repeatedly threw stones at him and threatened him with death. He said that belief has made him fearless and that he strives with all his soul to suffer for Christ. He calls himself a simple, modest Christian. 'I am a modest Christian. I cannot avoid acknowledging the existence of God when I see the starry heaven or sit at the grave of someone who was close to me or when I see how martyrs are executed.'

When we parted, Father Alexander whispered: 'I gather that you are people like Father Dimitrii Dudko or Father Gleb Yakunin. I listen to Western broadcasts every night. Keep strong and don't be afraid of anything!'

Sister Marusia

Our meeting with Sister Marusia also impressed us. We had just got to the village of Pechory. Obviously women could not be accommodated in a monastery. So we began to look for somewhere to spend the night. The village of Pechory has changed with time into a close, a clandestine monastery. Women living near the monastery secretly give lodging to pilgrims. Often there are house searches by the police and fines. But regardless of the severe penalties and threats, the inhabitants of the village welcome pilgrims from all over Russia. During our visit we slept in these 'monasteries' packed together on the floor in peasant huts, in attics and in stables, stalls and wood-stacks.

After knocking on the door of one of the houses I said in the manner of someone visiting a monastery, 'Lord Jesus Christ, Son of God, have mercy on me, a sinner.'

The answer came back, 'Amen.'

We went into the room. It was already full of people. But there was room for us in the hallway, next to a pilgrim, Marusia the servant of God.

As we noticed later, Marusia is a type that one often finds among the pilgrims from the ordinary people. She is fifty-eight years old, small, grey, a scarf on her head, and soft shoes on her feet. She cannot read or write. She has been a housewife and looked after children all her life. She lives in a village near Saransk.

In the winter she had a dream. She dreamed that she was eating human flesh. She couldn't swallow it, and it stuck in her mouth. She also saw a dead, bloated old woman in her dream. 'It was as if I were this woman,' she said.

This dream showed her that she had not been to communion for a long time. Here you must realize that the church was about twelve miles away from her village.

After a month she had another dream. She had ringworms in her mouth. She went to church and to communion, but she understood that that was not enough. 'Anyway, we all die one day.' She sold her herd, four animals. She paid the money into her savings account and hid the passbook under the floor of her house. Furniture, farm equipment, everything that she had saved up over long years of unceasing work for her old age were now a burden on her soul. Having given up all this, she became a pilgrim on the way to the holy places. She had already been four months on the road. With passionate conviction she said,

'Even if everything goes wrong and they knock down the houses there and everything for themselves, the house and the jewellery and the money, I don't care. What do I need that for? I've enough. It's time to go to God. I don't ever think of paradise. What would I do in paradise? As long as I at least get a place in hell, right on the edge.'

She had never once seen the Bible in her life. She asked whether it was a big book. She had only a vague knowledge of the content of the gospel, but knew that 'we need to gather up treasures for heaven'. And what she knew she tried to put into practice without delay. Like other pilgrim women, Marusia expected the end of the world. 'Look, the green leaves are falling in the middle of summer, the end is near.'

Or, 'Is it true that there will soon be war with China, as it says in the Bible?'

Since recently in Russia there had been a reform of passes and the population had been given new passes with a red cover, she asked, 'Can one accept the new passes? What

71

does it say about that in the Bible? I wouldn't be surprised if they were from the Antichrist!'

There were conversations among the women, greatly agitated that soon everyone would be converted to 'the Polish faith' (which is what they called Catholicism). These are echoes of the ecumenical congress which had recently been held in Moscow.

'But why are you afraid of Catholicism?' we asked Marusia.

'Why, because they only acknowledge Christ. But they don't worship the Queen of Heaven and the Holy Trinity, and they circumcise the men. The end has come. Have you heard there's an abomination in the churches in America? Women are becoming priests!'

Every day and every hour she prepared herself for the end of the world, and she thought that it would come at night.

She said to us, 'Why don't you sleep in nightdresses? The Lord will come and you'll appear before him in underwear.'

Among the monks and the worshippers nothing escapes her.

'Didn't you see how the monk looked at your long dress and said something?'

'This young deacon gazes around all over the place. He'll never make a monk.'

'You didn't stand properly all through the mass. Now on one foot, now on another. The devil probably put nuts under your feet. I was watching you all through the mass.'

'If the devil sits on your eyelids when you want to go to sleep, say a prayer: "Lord have mercy on me."'

'We've seen screaming women, the way the devil makes them bellow. Father Antonii rebuked them firmly and the devil went out into him. Now he's started to go around bellowing.'

Sister Marusia, who fearlessly gave up everything and followed God, is very anxious. She has heard a good deal about psychiatric hospitals and is very frightened because she did not bring the new red pass from her village. Without papers, a person does not exist in our country, and everyone knows that very well. Marusia was afraid that people would arrest her for vagrancy and being a parasite and put her in a psychiatric hospital. Anxiety banishes all other feelings from Marusia's belief. She is afraid above all of the Last Judgment, of which she speaks constantly. Firmly rooted in her consciousness is the idea that human beings are judged according to their merits. She hardly understands the idea of complete forgiveness: 'I hope only for the intercession of the most holy Queen.' The thought of the Mother of God raises her above the hopelessness of her expectation of the future.

We often heard her tell how a high official 'with flaps' (she meant the epaulettes on dress uniform) had his seven-year-old child buried unbaptized. He dreamed that the children were playing somewhere in a meadow, but his child was not with them. The general asked, 'Where's my child, then?''There,' he was told.

But the children were pointing to a kind of darkness that you can't see.

'Why aren't you playing with the other children?', the father asked.

'They won't let me in, I'm not baptized.'

After this dream the general had his other children and himself baptized and asked to be married to his wife in church. He told all that to a priest and added, 'Write to anyone you want, it makes no difference to me now.'

These women don't understand the word 'atheist'. They understand Communist and mean by it the worst enemy of religion. Sister Marusia often got upset and wept. She is capable of self-criticism: 'There used to be a woman who often told me that the priest never stretched out his hand to her to be kissed for the blessing. So after that I began to despise her. And when I went to the same priest to get the blessing, he didn't stretch out his hand for me to kiss either. So obviously I've sinned. You shouldn't despise anyone.'

The next day

Early in the morning, when it was hardly day, Marusia woke us: 'It's time for mass.' The inhabitants of the village and the pilgrims converged in droves for the morning liturgy. The liturgy was celebrated in the church of the Assumption of Mary, which is like a cave and mysterious and warm.

As soon as she entered the church a woman knelt down and cried out in a very loud voice (how could her voice be so loud?), 'My loves, do not be tempted because the godless are burning the icons. Do not be confused because our Orthodox churches are being razed to the ground and the godless have torn down the crosses of those which are still standing. Your heart must not be confused. Unless God wills it, my loves, not a single hair of your head will be lost. And do not be confused because all the priests have been killed. Now they are praying for us sinners before God in heaven. Speak, my loves, confess. If no priest is there, fall on your knees before an icon. Unburden your soul to the Mother of God, as you would have unburdened it to your earthly mother. She will never forsake you.'

The people thronged round the woman who was crying out. In the constant tranquillity of the monastery this scene was clearly unusual. Finally one of the older monks came past: 'Eudokia, get up, be silent and go to worship.'

The woman immediately obeyed, got up quietly and went into the church.

Father Feodorit

We also went in. We took our place in a long line for confession. Father Feodorit, a monk who was not all that old, with a serious, simple face, said a few words before the confession. He spoke of those who no longer knew how to behave properly in church. People should not walk around during mass, and it was wrong to kiss icons incessantly. People had to look directly at the icons, 'face to face'. When the Gospel was read out, people had to stand still because the King of Kings was entering the church. As soon as the reading of the Gospel began, some people would start to cough, because Satan specially waited for this significant moment to do damage.

At the confession many people complained that they constantly got angry and fought with their drunken husbands. Father Feodorit said, 'If you fight, that means that you will be serving the devil just as much as this drunkard. So afterwards your husband will drink even more. It is better to pray and the devil will go away.'

The pilgrim

I had noticed him the day before, the first time I had come into the church. He was a small and very confused man. It was evident to look at him that he had had a difficult and laborious life. His head and face were covered with black, close-cut and bristly hair and his arms were full of tattoos. In his hands he held a shopping bag with bread and a jug of water. He too had only just come.

In the church he went past all the icons one by one. With deep feeling he put his mouth against each, and kept kissing it, evidently without looking at what was depicted on the icon. 'Why are you kissing that?', said a women. 'That's hell.' 'Oh,' said the pilgrim, laughing and quite indifferent, 'it's all the same to me.'

When he heard of another pilgrim and the torments that this pilgrim had had in a psychiatric clinic because of his faith, he got angry at his tormentor. His language sounded convinced and passionate. 'Don't worry! God, the Lord, knows your deeds. A terrible fate awaits you. Have you heard of the Bermuda triangle? Ships and planes get lost there every day. None of them has ever been found. And recently 80,000 people were killed in Romania. But that's not all, you'll see.'

He accepted all believers with absolute love as his brothers and sisters, and showed respect to the monks. In his exaltation he tried to kiss their hands.

Brother Dimitrii

We saw him for the first time standing beside the springs with the holy water in the courtyard of the monastery. Brother Dimitrii looked like a peasant; he was short, and middle-aged. He wore a patched robe, a shabby jacket, wide breeches and a hat. His worn face was like that of a lonely person, someone who has suffered a great deal.

When we came up to Dimitrii, he pretended to be someone being made to take tablets in a psychiatric clinic. He opened his mouth and showed that the tablets were no longer there, that he had swallowed them. Then suddenly he spat them out again. At the request of the pilgrims he demonstrated this method once again, swallowed a 'raspberry' and spat it out again a few seconds later, rather like a circus trick. Then he showed how to make one's whole body shake in order to prevent having an injection. He had acquired his bitter knowledge by spending ten years all told in psychiatric clinics, in which he had been put because of his faith. Later he gave us a piece of paper on which he had written his sorry history. He had obviously rewritten it several times, but he could not bring it to an end. Here it is.

For twenty-five years I lived stupidly. Then after my time in the army, I was thought to be a fool. I was punished in this way for my simple faith. God called me in this way. He has constantly whispered to me and taught me. Human language has no words to express all the seriousness and bitterness of that cup of suffering which I have drunk in accordance with the will of my heavenly Father – for the sake of truth and righteousness.

76

Life has no joy for me and it is difficult because I love the truth and have done no evil. It is nothing but lasting torment and trials. I have not experienced life, I couldn't marry. I have not travelled around, since God has not given me the time for that. Ten years in psychiatric clinics – that is what he has called me to. He has never left me in the lurch in torments and severe suffering. After military service between 1953 and 1956 it pleased God to work a miracle in me. After the army I got a driving licence for a motor bicycle. One year and three months after passing the driving test God persuaded me to practise motor-cycle racing and study the principle of the motor. But I still did not have a motor bicycle of my own. From childhood onwards I had wanted to be involved with technical things. After my first training it pleased God to let me become city champion.

Sunday 18 May 1958 was a working day in the spirit factory of the city of Biisk. I worked there for seven months in all, and during my time there I gained experience, passed examinations and made progess. I rose to being a mechanic and finally an electrician; of the five jobs I tried, electrician was most to my taste; there was fresh air and the work is very simple, but it was not resolved that I should work at that for long. On 18 May…

This is where the report by brother Dimitrii breaks off abruptly. He could never bring himself to write how on Sunday 18 May his way of the cross began, how the First Aid came and how strong orderlies, bursting with health and strength, easily reduced him to the last circle of hell: the psychiatric clinic, where people have no rights and where gradually the brain is destroyed, the soul tortured and the body fatally poisoned.

The startsy

The *startsy* are the pride of the monastery. The fame of their perception, their wisdom and holiness extends all over

Russia. From Kazakhstan and Siberia, from the north and from the Ukraine, people go to the *startsy*. Many come simply to be blessed by them, others just to see them. It is hard to have a conversation with a *starets*, so many people want to come to them, so large is the crowd of people that surrounds them wherever they appear. Even before my conversion I had heard from my yoga friends of great gurus, whom they called Fr Yakov and Father Antonii (the names of the *startsy* have been changed), the famous *startsy* of the monastery of Pechory. The *startsy* talked with everyone, even the yoga practitioners; in a marvellous way they have understood that in the conditions of modern Russia the ways to God are becoming even more unfathomable than before. For many of us yoga was the first step to Christ.

Father Tikhon

Father Tikhon was the first *starets* whom I succeeded in seeing. After a long service in the little wooden church in a convent near Riga, and a modest meal together in the refectory of the convent, people went to the little house of Archimandrite Tikhon. Earlier I had heard the most unusual things about this eighty-year-old *starets*. I had been told how when he was young he had fallen in the water. He had already sunk to the river bed and nevertheless continued to pray, his hands in the form of a cross on his breast. Because of the high level of the water in the spring the river had burst its banks; the turbulent flood hurled him out again and he was saved. Like almost all the other *startsy* Father Tikhon has spent long years in camps and prisons – people said twenty-five years in all. They said that in the camp he found time for the daily service despite the inhuman conditions which are imposed to destroy people. He got up an hour earlier than everyone else and celebrated mass silently for himself. In the evening he cleared up for the other prisoners – he was imprisoned with thieves – and no one ever heard a reproach from him. He never asked anyone

78

for support and never tried to exercise any influence in what he said. The women in the convent told me that the majority of these criminals who had been in prison with Father Tikhon were firm believers when they were released.

Outside the Archimandrite's little house there was a long line of people. There were not just ordinary women but artists from Moscow and two or three hippies with large crosses hanging on their chests.

I was lucky – the *starets* found enough time to receive me before Vespers. I had only just become a Christian. I did not really know what kind of one, an Orthodox, a Catholic or a Lutheran, so insignificant did all these difference seem to me. But apart from that I had a mass of other questions and doubts. I still knew very little about Christianity. It was inappropriate to keep the *starets* long, so I chose one of the questions which tormented me most.

'In your sermon you spoke all the time about the fear of God. But why should we fear? The whole earth is full of the praise of the Lord, and has not God the Lord himself said that the prince of this world is driven out? Have we not then finally been delivered from evil?'

Father Tikhon's answer amazed me: 'You're thinking like Adam in paradise. You haven't yet become a real Christian because you haven't understood that the true Christian chooses the way of the cross and the supreme joy consists in bearing the cross of Christ. But don't be in a hurry: in time all that will be clear to you.'

And indeed very soon the initial euphoria I experienced as a new convert was in fact put to unexpected tests. At that time I began to accept suffering as openly as the joy which God had given me in such abundance. And the words of the gospel became clear to me: 'My yoke is easy and my burden is light.'

The *startsy* are real doctors. I have never heard empty and flattering words from them. The medicine that they give is often bitter, but it always works. No one goes away from a *starets* in a state of despair or even sadly. All leave them comforted, with bright and rejuvenated faces. Not only is their spiritual and psychological wisdom evident, but also the power of their prayer, the power of the concrete, specific love that is felt by everyone who comes to meet them. There is also the boundless trust that the people have in them. Thousands and thousands of people in Russia live on their memory of having spoken with the *starets* and of the instructions he gave them. The *starets* is the icon of God. Even if one has seen him only once, one realizes that it is wrong to go on living as before, that from this moment on the correctness of everything in one's life must be tested in the light of this beauty and blessedness. In the person of the *starets*, holiness becomes summons and demand. My friend once said, 'If *Starets* Yakov is like that, what must Christ be like?'

Starets Yakov, from whom love streamed, was followed by an enormous crowd of people whenever he appeared. People felt in a very tangible way the richness of the blessing that emanated from him. That sometimes amounted to a pagan fetishism: many pressed round the *starets* to touch his garments. They said that a spiritual power also went out from that.

Obviously the *startsy* themselves fought against such idolatry of their persons. Humility is their main characteristic. *Starets* Yakov often said of himself, 'I am a mat under people's feet.' And again, 'I always want to get on a bench, but I find myself under it. I want to be on it, but it falls on me. And so I keep clambering up again without getting tired.'

As a priest Father Yakov had a great spiritual breadth. I

and other 'intellectual' believers who regarded ourselves as extremely tolerant people and were not surprised at anything were amazed at the breadth of the *startsy's* perspectives: a breadth in which there was no kind of liberalism or indifference. Evidently, like their courage, this was the result of inner tranquillity, an inner power and trust in God.

Father Yakov had an unusually great understanding of suffering. I recall how once after the service in the Church of the Assumption we stood in a long line to get the holy blessing and to kiss his hand. Then a man entered the church. He was my friend Nikolai, who had come with me in the bus to Pechory. I knew his sorry fate. He had broken with the world, which for him was full of unresolved tragic conflicts in his family and his work. The feeling of catastrophe and forsakenness stood out on his tired young face. This face was in the most marked contrast to the other restful and reconciled faces of people after a long service. Nikolai uncertainly joined the end of the long line to recieve the blessing. But the *starets* immediately noticed him, went up to him – he was seeing him for the first time – put his arms around him and kissed him on the forehead, the cheeks and the back of the neck, in the way a mother might kiss a hurt child. He asked Nikolai where he had come from and when he could come to him to confession. When I think back on this scene, my own heart seems to me to be no longer Christian but rough and made of stone.

In the time that followed I felt in myself the power of the love which emanated from this *starets*. From my conversation with him I had the feeling of boundless reconciliation with the whole world, a reconciliation which embraced not only human beings but also animals and stones. At that time I became aware how the Holy Spirit is called the Comforter. It was the Holy Spirit who was with us then. The *starets* spoke sternly and without equivocation about my failings, about my haste and immaturity, but I went

81

away from him comforted and feeling as though I had been in paradise. I recall that he did not conceal his concern to give comfort. In his conversation with me he kept saying, 'Well now, how else can I comfort you?' His love was so great, but also so tender and so strong, that I was not afraid to speak quite openly with him and to tell him all that oppressed me. In conversation, it seemed to me he respected every blade of grass. For example, he did not say 'apple', but used the diminutive. He himself was a person permeated with God and renewed, and the whole world around him began to resound, filled with divine harmony and power.

There were no generalizations in the answers which *Starets* Yakov gave. Whatever the way in which he approached people, it was forthright and specific. 'Everyone has his own way to God, everyone must give in accordance with his measure,' I heard him say. I recall how he was speaking with some women in my presence; they had come to ask a blessing from him. The question of marriage and divorce has become very dramatic in our difficult times in Russia. There is hardly a single marriage which one could term normal or regard as successful. And half the marriages in the country end in divorce. Therefore the *startsy* do not give their blessings too quickly. Father Yakov asked one of the women who asked for a blessing: 'Could you give birth to a saint? If you are prepared to and can, then marry; if not, I shall not bless you.'

He said to another: 'You are a learned woman, and science has always been the most important thing of all for you. But marriage calls for many sacrifices. Will you be able to give up your academic activities in order to spend a great deal of your time on things that you will find boring: everyday life, shopping, washing? And when your children are born you will unavoidably have to make such a sacrifice. Think about that.'

He spoke like that with everyone, depending on their inner make-up.

Father Yakov was fond of saying to us new converts, 'Get ready for the long journey, don't be in a hurry.' At the same time he was demanding, he was very concerned that there should be spiritual progress and that his spiritual children should win one victory after another.

Father Antonii

Father Antonii is an exorcist known throughout Russia. He is thin, small, very grey. But he is not a particularly old monk, not yet sixty. People come to the monastery from all over the country, the possessed, maniacs, and ordinary sick people. It is interesting that in ordinary everyday life these maniacs and possessed people are no different from anyone else. But in the monastery they show both sides: the best in them and the worst. These unfortunate people are usually women. There are also men, but fewer of them. In the world many of them feel a constant, intolerable, oppressive heaviness. This feeling drives them to seek liberation in the monasteries. Sometimes one hears loud howling and screaming during the liturgy in the monastery at Pechory: some growl like animals, others keep throwing themselves to the ground, and yet others burst out into blasphemies in their rage. It is not easy to take a woman screaming like that to communion – a few people hold her using all their strength. I have constantly been amazed at the complete tranquillity of the priest administering the communion. He seems 'like someone with power', like a doctor, like a victor. After receiving the holy gifts the screaming women usually calm down, their faces become soft and gentle, and many of them weep silently.

Twice a week Father Antonii does exorcisms. Outsiders are not admitted. The *starets* reads special prayers for several hours. A young monk helped him on those days. All the rest – there were about twenty people in church – had come as patients to the *starets*. To begin with, those who were possessed cried out, spat at the *starets*, and writhed on the floor. But gradually some of them became weaker and others began to help the *starets*, put up candles, prayed together.

According to Soviet law there is such a thing as illegal healing. Anyone who heals without a diploma or any medical credentials is strictly punished. According to what I heard in the monastery the police had beaten Father Antonii severely on several occasions, almost to death. 'The devil's revenge,' it was said. He was brutally hit in the eyes in the presence of other monks. 'Why didn't you stand up for him, then?' A monk replied: 'It is not in the nature of monks to interfere in God's work. Father Antonii wanted to accepted suffering and he was ready to take it.'

Father Alipii

Father Alipii is the president of the monastery. He often stood on the balcony of his little house. And he acted a little like a fool in Christ. He would often talk from his balcony to people who came. His knowledge of people was infallible. A young woman went up to the balcony, well dressed, eyes lowered: 'Bless me, Father Alipii, I want to enter the convent.'

'You enter the convent? I won't bless you.'

And then, in a shocked way: 'Go into hospital as a nurse. You'll drink, you'll begin to complain, but such work will save you. A convent will ruin you. I will not bless you.'

Tourist groups often look round the monastery. They think they are visiting a cultural monument, and want to see the exotic nature of a monk's life. These tourists are usually disconcerted. Many of them are afraid that they are in quite a different world; it is interesting for them, but they don't know to whom they should turn, whom they could ask; they have no background for knowing how they should behave, how they should look round and could talk in these unaccustomed conditions. Compared with the beauty of the measured movements of the monks these hasty tourists look absurd and lost. One can see that some of them are ashamed of their curiosity. Others, not many, act in a provocative way. Meeting young believers like my friend and me put them in a rage. How is it possible that in the age of science and the cosmos young people with intelligent faces cross themselves in the monastery, genuflect and cover their heads with scarves? They have completely lost their senses. Some particularly unruly tourists are eager to take up the battle with this religious trickery. The monks are silent, they go about as usual, but the head of the monastery, Father Alipii, is not disinclined to talk to atheists. 'Aren't you ashamed to look people in the eye?' shouted one of the militant atheist women. 'You're parasites. You feed at the expense of the people. Whose bread are you eating?'

'But we're also the people,' replied Father Alipii calmly, 'you can't separate us from the people. For example, fifteen of our monks fought in the Great War. So did I.'

Of course Father Alipii did not try to excuse himself to this woman by saying that nowadays the monasteries give sixty per cent of their income to the state. They pay tax, and the state, which is separate from the church, can only be envious of how well the monastery economy is organized, how the monks go to work with prayer and zeal, how the pilgrims think that helping in the work of the monastery is supreme bliss. Whole villages in the hungry countryside are provided with food from the monastery kitchens.

Father Alipii is also an artist. He is very fond of creative young people. Our religious artists go to him to get his advice and receive his blessing. Yesterday's pagans and sceptics, those who once rejected any moral norm and authority, now speak with reverence and lowered voices the name of Father Alipii.

From the Diary of an Emigrant

Prelude

It began almost a year ago. In September 1979 we formed the first unofficial, free women's movement. It all began with the founding of the journal *Woman and Russia*, which has now been translated into many European and non-European languages and which first brought the growing movement to the attention of the world. For the first time, after sixty years of silence, Russian women were beginning to talk about their problems. A Western journal, of course pro-Soviet, remarked, not without some irony: 'The Russian women are not speaking, they are howling.' And that was not wrong: the weeping, sighing and lamenting of tormented women found expression in our newspaper. Of course there were also attempts at theoretical or objective discussions, but the dominant factor was an immediacy which also made the journal so lively. Women were beginning to speak in an open and informed way about things of which people in the country stubbornly kept quiet: the cruelty of life, which was perverted into a daily battle to stay alive; the stifling atmosphere and the pressure of high-rise dwellings; the desperate state of so-called free medical care; the collapse of families; prostitution in the Soviet Union and much, much else.

The journal *Woman and Russia* was a bombshell. Women's problems formed the focal point for various converging lines, taking up a whole series of issues, major and minor. Women's suffering is the most specific, the most evident and the most demanding. And women among us suffer

86

twice if not three times as much as men. They work like men, since families cannot get by on one wage. They are plagued by their homes, which in the Soviet Union have nothing attractive about them. One need only add to this drunkenness, standing in line everywhere, increasing hunger – and the picture of an involuntary martyr will emerge: the picture of the simple Russian woman.

However, we were concerned with more than these social questions. Almost all the women in the movement which had been newly formed were believing Christians. So the movement was called 'Mary'. We saw that social changes would not liberate either men or women unless they were connected with the main thing, with the spiritual revolution which was taking place in every soul and throughout society. We said that women could only be free in the church. The editors of the women's journal had also been very well known to the KGB earlier: Julia Voznesenskaya, Natalia Malakhovskaya, Tatiana Mamonova and myself. Before that we had been persecuted, watched and arrested. But with the appearance of *Woman and Russia* the real persecution began. Thanks to the support of women in the West, especially women who had quite a different programme, namely the feminists, they did not wipe us out in the first days. Our group existed for a whole year and was active: we called women's conferences, continued to edit the newspaper, protested against the war in Afghanistan, helped all that we could.

A week before the beginning of the Olympic games in Moscow we were given a choice: imprisonment or emigration. We chose the West. So on 20 July 1980 we, the first founders of the women's movement, arrived in Vienna. But our place was immediately taken by other Christian women, and it has proved impossible to wipe out the women's movement. It was the wish of my father confessor that I should emigrate and not go to prison, and he gave me

87

his blessing. So emigration was also an expression of my obedience to the church.

Outside

29 July 1980

I had arrived in Vienna. What did I feel? Was it a feeling of freedom? No! I was also free in Russia. Freedom is a gift of God. That is obligation, not a duty. I had the feeling that I had come into a world of forms. Everything in this world found expression, every sense had excellent packaging. Everything here sought to please, was in a hurry to serve people in some way. The way in which in the Western order human beings stand at the centre, this form of anthropomorphism, amazed me greatly.

In Russia we have to spend at least half our energy overcoming a thousand obstacles which are connected with our nonsensical and difficult way of life: noise in the streets, crowds in the shops, lines outside the food shops, the battle to travel on public transport, the general coarseness and greed – you don't have these difficulties here. But there are others: there are so many beautiful things, things that are attractive, that one is not sufficiently attentive to heaven.

1 August 1980

The first interviews, correspondents. Hardly had we got into the West than there were continual public appearances. I spoke in enormous rooms and there were enthusiastic audiences, there was applause. It is not long since I was in Leningrad, every day expecting to be beaten up on the street, to be hurled into a car or taken off to the mental hospital. It seems only yesterday that student friends with whom I had taken the same courses ran away from me and went over to the other side of the street; that my parents were ashamed of me.

But here I can see none of that sort of thing. I am only

terribly tired, would like to go to sleep, breathe the air of Vienna. The questions which are put to me are all the same: 'When did the women's movement begin in Russia? How does it differ from Western feminism? What did the 1917 revolution bring for the Russian woman? What are your plans for the future?'

After a number of press conferences of a general kind journalists came from various newspapers and magazines. How eager I was for Catholics to come, Protestants, someone from my fellow believers! But no one did. Above all we were besieged by feminists. Very nice women, understanding, independent, radical. It amazed me that these sympathetic people called themselves witches. How strange it was to see the generous and open face of the American poetess Robin and to be told, 'I'm a witch.'

Of course they read no religious significance into this remark; they were attracted by the martyr ideal of these unfortunate women who were burned by the Inquisition. It was their view that these were the 'progressive' women of their time, doctors, midwives, that they listened to the voice of nature, that they were nearer to the cosmos. As for psychology, those of us who came from Russia even liked the Western feminist type. In their struggle to carry things through, in their fearless contempt for the conventions of public opinion, they showed infectious courage and creativity.

The main topic of conversation and the topic which also sparked off a dispute with the feminists was Christianity. And here I had to work quite hard to show how our Russian feminism had an immediate religious character and why the modern Russian woman finds freedom and consolation, power for life and bold action, only in the church.

With us, so far only the church has been concerned with the 'women's question'. Only the Russian clergy solve the deep problems of nurture, unhappy marriages, abortions and alcoholism. Nowadays ninety per cent of those who go to church in Russia are women. I try to tell my Western friends that, that the church is the most living thing in the world, that it is the mystical body of Christ. But they just have no inkling about mysticism any more. In addition I try to explain things to them in the perspective of a particular idea of personality. I talk about Christianity in terms of existentialism and psychoanalysis, say that in Christianity we have overcome our infancy and one-sidedness and have become mature people with full worth.

I note that for them Christianity is no more than a codex of moral regulations and a system of prohibitions. They understand even the Most Holy Lady as a moral abstraction to instil fear, the very one who is so near to us and so akin to us.

And there is my good fortune – to speak of the Mother of God to people who have long since stopped wanting to hear about Christianity. To speak of her with love where she has been changed into a dead moral ideal, where people do not recall her or fear her. Could I ever have dreamed that?

Of course so far I have hardly succeeded in convincing the Western feminists. But it is also a good thing that they should see how effective Christianity is in practice, that they should see that it is successful in standing up to resistance. And perhaps God the Lord will also reveal to them what we regard as the ideal of the women which stands above all courage and heroism: in the words of I Peter, 'the hidden person of the heart with the imperishable jewel of a gentle and quiet spirit'.

20 August 1980

I saw my first religious broadcast ever on the television. I thank God that we have atheism and no religious education. What this man said on the screen was likely to drive more people out of the church than the clumsy chatter of our paid atheists. Dressed up in a posh way, the self-satisfied preacher had to talk of love. But the way in which he presented himself excluded any possibility of a sermon. It would have even got in the way of a simple conversation with another person. He was a boring bad actor with mechanical and studied gestures. He was faceless. For the first time I understood how dangerous it is to talk about God.

Each word must be a sacrifice – filled to the brim with authenticity. Otherwise it is better to keep silent.

5 September 1980

The carefully tended, spectacular beauty, the joyful and resounding beauty of Europe, flew past the windows of the coach. I thought again of our roads, the little railway stations, landscapes with a lowering sky and endless neglected fields, with refuse by the side of the road, with torn, uncultivated earth, orphaned, and so akin to our state of mind.

By contrast Europe... To the eyes of a Russian there seems to be little room, but on the other hand there is no constriction either. The Alps, the flowers, the woods, everything seems to me to be much more beautiful than the pictures I've seen. But a wounded heart takes everything wrongly: the more beautiful the landscapes through the windows of my coach, the more piercing the grief within me. Lermontov's words came to mind: 'Life is like a banquet at a strange festival.'

All through the month I've been seeing around me faces which are always laughing, which are all lovable, full of good will, ready to help. But there is bitterness in my soul. Suddenly I think of Misha's face. The recollection is very vivid in my mind. Misha is someone whom I often visited in the psychiatric clinic in Leningrad. He had recently become a Christian. The neighbours in his block had put him in the hospital. Fortunately it is an open clinic and not a prison, and on Sundays it is possible to visit the sick. All the last Sundays I spent with Misha. They had begun to

91

stuff him full of drugs, in other words, slowly to kill him. This young man with bright eyes who was once so alive was now an ageless person with a thin, blunt face and an immovable, indifferent look. His face will stay in my mind for a long time as a recollection of that other world where there is blatant evil, where it is impossible not to react to suffering. Here even the food people put in front of me confuses me. Everything is so tasty, varied; there is much that I am eating for the first time. And again recollections of Russia are a silent reproach. Hunger in the provinces, children without milk and vegetables, grumbling long lines, standing there for all the basic essentials.

And our old people! Here a woman of fifty looks quite young. I'm always getting ages wrong. For us that would be an old woman. The bodies of Russian women are either bloated with illness or unnaturally thin; men are prematurely grey and can no longer speak because of an excessive consumption of vodka; sick children – for the first time in all these years of happy and gentle Christianity the pain of the memory burned up so strongly in me that I felt anger towards those who know all about this. They know how 'normally' people live in the West and they know how they live with us. Those who kill people deliberately by turning what was once the richest land into a wilderness. One modern writer said, 'Russian suffering must disturb the contentment of the world.'

7 October 1980

What a mysterious thing freedom is! It's like the air. People only begin to value it when they lose it. I can see that Western people, too, are barely free. And the main thing is that there is little desire for freedom.

Here nihilism shows itself in a different way and not as with us. As an example, yesterday my train arrived in the station of the great German city of Frankfurt. An enormous station, and above it a gigantic illumination: the letters MM.

I asked my companion, 'What's that? Some special symbol, a slogan, something significant?'

She replied, 'It's just an advertisement for champagne.'

And everything is dominated by the burdensome commercial world. For example in the cinema. People talk with such mysterious and suggestive voices about trivia, washing powder, some kind of brushes, as if they were the most important and indispensable things.

And here even the priests are ashamed to talk about other things which are in fact indispensable to everyone – the soul, the meaning of life, redemption. Truly it's a perverse and distorted world.

I recall a priest whom I met a short while ago. I had gone on a trip which was organized by the congregation of a village. The young and energetic minister, a sporty type, talked the whole weekend. During the two days which we spent on the coach he talked about anything that people wanted, about aeroplanes and football, about the elections and about the food. He laughed a lot, above all tried to keep everyone cheerful. Rather like our popular entertainers. And all the time out through the windows was a world which was unexpectedly beautiful, with steep cliffs, lit with deep blue, violet, almost other-worldly colours so that I was quite naturally reminded of one of the psalms: 'How wonderful are your works, O God; with great wisdom you have created all things.'

Later, when we got back, I asked the priest, 'Why didn't you once say anything about God? Why didn't you talk about the beauty of his world?' He replied, 'If I begin to talk of God I lose all my people, and get left alone.'

'But loneliness was never a sin,' I said, and thought that it was not true that he would lose people. How the country people had listened to me when I talked to them about our church, about the church, about prayer! And they asked me for more and more!

25 December 1980

Here for the first time I heard questions from journalists like, 'Why don't you want to become priests?'

I must say that to a Russian Orthodox woman this question sounds mad. Why has our feminism never seen the problem? I must first look for an answer. The words of the Lord automatically come to mind, 'And let him who would be first among you be your servant.' In our churches there is no talk of the problem of earthly equality or inequality. There the laws are quite different. There is heaven which has come down to earth. Our women treat the priests with reverence, but they also understand the responsibility which every priest has towards God and humanity. Women are of the view that the cross of a priest is harder than the cross of a woman who has no spiritual consecration and that it is easier to be saved if one has a simple, insignificant position. And there is another saying which applies to our women in the church who are even now rescuing the church: 'God has chosen the foolish of the world to put to shame the wise, and he has chosen the weak of the world to put to shame the strong, and the insignificant of the world and the lowly and whatever has no significance, has God chosen to bring significance.'

26 December 1980

Today I spoke in a church for the first time in my life. It was in a gigantic cathedral dedicated to Mary. When Father F. invited me to say a few words before mass, I became terribly confused. Could I ever have imagined such an honour, to speak in church, to preach in the house of the Lord? But, as Father F. had asked, and in order to obey him, I plucked up courage and spoke. I spoke in German, and God the Lord gave me the words and the power to tell of our Russian church which is going the blessed and royal way of the cross. I spoke of our miraculous conversion to God, and said that 'God the Lord could even make children of Abraham out of stones.' I wanted to convey to my audience a sense of the miracle so that they could feel the degree, indeed the boundlessness of our gratitude to God, but I still feel myself unexpectedly saved – and not according to my merits – rescued by God from a terrible, fatal illness.

3 February 1981

Is it possible that emigration has set me back? Sometimes I cry to God, Please don't let me lose my existence, my soul, here; God grant that emptiness and boredom do not kill me. And *I* pray for that, I who once regarded both romanticism and poetic 'follies' as immature, I who had discovered in Christianity the supreme realism and who was ashamed of my former predilections, as I thought them to be pagan, who once even rejected Dostoevsky, since he seemed to me to be too 'hysterical' and not to correspond to the 'sobriety' of true belief. And all that not out of snobbery, nor out of the exalted zeal of a new convert. In fact I saw that nihilism is offensive, that it is laughable and even tasteless. After the liturgy all Romantic literature and modern culture appeared to me in everyday dress, caught up in simple self-contemplation and emptiness. After Jesus, the sweetest of all, any bread seemed to me to be coarse and tasteless. Where then has this taste now disappeared to?

As before, I live by prayer; as at that time I go into church with a feeling of inner exaltation, and indeed as though I were coming home. But there in Russia the whole of life was full to the brim, it was intensive and more unruly. There was no emptiness in it and despite the external difficulties the underlying tone was cheerfulness; cheerfulness which goes with liberation: cheerfulness which made us invulnerable. Russia today is going through the ninth circle of hell and at the same time the luckiest people in the world live in it.

95

4 March 1981

There are no beggar women in the churches here but people who are dressed well and tastefully. It seems even strange to me to see them in church. One also sees many men here, another great difference from Russia. But one soon notices that everyone's attitude is somehow not an attitude of prayer. The majority stand there absent-minded and indifferent, hands crossed on their chest. Only curious tourists stand around in Russian churches like that nowadays. Recently when I was talking here to Russian emigrants I told them sharply, 'In our churches only KGB people stand like that.' A woman retorted, 'But we've been to church since childhood, we're used to it.'

Yesterday I heard even more amazing words in a sermon by a Russian priest, an emigrant. 'We who visit church...' One does not *live* in the church. One visits it. That is something that I could never have imagined, that people can get used to church. It shows that the church can become the most boring institution in the world. It shows that one can dissolve into banality the miracle of faith that moves mountains and raises the dead.

But nevertheless it is the church. And I shall love it. I'm now trying to love the well-to-do and self-satisfied church, which is in all things opposed to what proves to be the original idea of the church.

Perhaps this 'nakedness' of the church here is of some use to me, now I'm going into a church which has no outward splendour. Now I go straight to God and talk directly to him. But in Russia often you had a kind of proud feeling, looking at yourself from outside: you're standing in the church so people look at you like a hero, as though you were a new person. It is now fashionable to be in the church just as it was once fashionable to be a revolutionary. Of course it's a good fashion. There is also the attraction of the good. Nevertheless, it is a fashion. There is something disturbing there. Every fashion is also a mask, a deceptive appearance, and in the gospel it says that such people have their reward. I'm glad that my faith has lost its outward splendour now that I'm an emigrant. The way to God must be hidden, and God who sees what is hidden will reveal it. In the West the church, any church, regardless of tradition, is steeped in emptying, *kenosis*, and it is hard to imagine anything deeper than that.

The best people are constantly pressing towards the fettered, immovable church in Russia which does not react to the world, which has no kind of advertisement or apologetics. But regardless of its giant efforts to keep pace with the times the church in the West is losing an increasing number of people. It is as though its spirit and power had fled. Difficult times have dawned for the church in the West, more difficult than for the church in the East. Everywhere the church is going the way of the cross. Only in Russia can it be seen that the cross is conquering. Here, however, everything is concealed and cannot be recognized.

21 March 1981

Eureka! I have the solution. Not those who have seen but those who believe are more blessed than those who have seen and then believe. So even the authentic Christians in the West must be more blessed than those of us who have come to faith in Russia. There, like Thomas, we have seen his wounds and touched concretely and visibly his now immortal body. We felt God, and we understood that he is more real than all the world around us.

But here I meet hardly anyone with a comparable experience. And nevertheless I have met true believers.

2 April 1981

I was at the church congress in Hamburg. The superficiality of the young people and their attitude, which virtually amounted to political agitation, amazed me and I found it unpleasant. It's called a church day. But how little talk there was of faith and the church! It was as if I were at a great meeting of Young Communists of the kind that could take place in the Soviet Union only in the first years after the revolution. It was difficult to make out human faces in the mass, to make out human voices behind the cries and thoughts behind the words. On this congress I made the acquaintance of German pacifism. The concern and the will to fight for peace are certainly good and important in themselves. Everyone wants peace. But for Russian Christians it is clear that there can be no outward peace without inner peace and inner freedom. St Seraphim Sarovki said, 'If you have inner peace, thousands of people will be saved around you.' But here these young people are obviously not talking of such a life but simply of staying alive. For me it was painful to hear Christians saying, 'Better red than dead'.

How much the opposite that is to everything that is now happening among Russian young people. There are those who are ready to lose their physical life in order that their soul and spirit do not die. It is a pity that the West today does not understand the value of suffering, its power to renew and purge; that it does not understand that the main thing is not the question of physical pain or even death, but the question of meaning. The martyrs who gave their life for Christ glowed with joy. And the experience of the persecuted Russian church says to us quite clearly that suffering for God does not take us away from him but on the contrary brings us nearer to him. The beginning of totalitarianism for me is where personality gets lost. It can also be buried under activism and unrest.

2 May 1981

I see that many Russian emigrants, yesterday's dissidents, hot, tired, tense people, seem lost, defeated and desolate here in the West. They have given up resisting against their outward environment, and the inner fire has disappeared. That is the flaw in merely heroic people; to live they need an enemy, they need a boundary situation, risk, standing on the periphery. I also loved all that but at the same time I am ashamed of it because God descends into the heart which is purified of passion: God, the still light.

Nietzsche says that 'All greatness is born in silence.'

10 May 1981

However difficult this unaccustomed world may be, I am grateful to God for allowing me to change my life completely. I am on another planet, and not only must my understanding be renewed, freed of old clichés and patterns, but also my body. It must even forget former smells, colours, expectations. It must detach itself from things that have become familiar, from being a defence mechanism, the certain refuge of my laziness and egoism. It must break with the sweet world of remembrance, of home, of the mother's womb. I must again become defenceless, as I was in the first days of my Christianity. Defenceless, that means needing God.

A void surrounds emigrants. Flowers without smell, people without faces, trees without names. One must become someone different, a monk, to accept and love the Martian world around. One must live with uninterrupted prayer. That is certain. Unless God comes down into this empty space all is up with humanity. In these months my God has come nearer than he was before.

And I have a reliable support, the church. And the blessing of my father confessor who said before I emigrated, 'Remember, you are not in exile. You are sent on a mission.'

Emigration confronts people with the decision either to go under in complete emptiness – and how many unhappy emigrants there are, even people who commit suicide – or to overcome nihilism through love. I noticed that if I have stillness and light in my heart, everything around me again becomes living and vivid. Even the stony Frankfurt skyscrapers begin to breathe, live in a new and bold dynamic. I can even converse with them.

7 May 1983

Today is Good Friday. It's evening and I've just got back from church. It was one of the most incomprehensible and most profound services of the year. We sang 'By the waves of the sea', the song of the waves which swallowed up the Egyptian Pharaoh. In fact, or symbolically, it is about the end of the rule of the princes of this world. Yesterday the place resounded with words of the Lord which have so seized my spirit and taken my breath away: 'Now is this world judged, now will the prince of this world be cast out.' That is what is now happening so openly and so simply; our tormentor has no more power over us.

And how much he has tormented me all this time and used my stupid pride, my unreasonable heart and my laziness to do that! I found the lectures particularly hard. Now I've already been appearing for almost three years, I give lectures, see hundreds, indeed thousands, of people. But I haven't got used to it. Last time I was in southern Austria and went into a number of small towns there. First I went to the painters' village of W. The Alps all around, the clear rustling brooks, the churches with their high domes, it all seemed to me unreal, toy, oppressive, in my heaviness and loneliness. The close honeyed warmth of the summer was already lying on the air, and it was so still that the whirring of a beetle seemed to be the loudest noise. It was Sunday, and now and then on the way I met happy couples, at ease with themselves and the world. My destination was the main church, where I wanted to drive out my heaviness with prayer. This heaviness is incomprehensible. It may be because I am an emigrant and people have torn the skin from my body, that is to say my homeland, my roots, my language and all material surroundings. Or also that I am afraid of speaking, overcoming my heavy, immovable 'subjectivity' and approaching fellow human beings, indeed telling them of very sublime, dangerous and responsible things: of the holy fire which once touched my heart in Russia, of the witnesses of faith, of holiness as the only way to oneself and God. Can I, who in my inexplicable sorrow now try to turn into a mouse and run away, can I appear in this way before people and tell them of such things? All that is clearly a temptation.

I'm beginning to hate not only myself but also these people. Given their 'bourgeois' character one can understand the mood of the left-wing people, since it is indeed very difficult for those with another temperament and different values to live in this sleepy and boring world.

I go into the church and read the notices: renovation of the façade, advice for the family, keep fit, men's gymnastics and finally, 'The Spiritual Resurrection of Russia, T.Goricheva.' I'm in good company.

So that's what the church is occupied with. I get even sadder. Why am I here? But it was time for my lecture, the room was full to bursting. The most varied people had come, young and old, learned and simple and – as I later discovered – people from the left and the right, feminists and nuns.

I prayed, crossed myself and began to speak; my gloomy mood disappeared and soon I saw hundreds of pairs of eyes directed towards me and I got to like more and more all these people who were continuing to pay attention. They had come to hear something about the Russian church and about Russia generally, Russia which at the same time attracts and terrifies, arouses hopes and anxieties and is still mysterious. And once I see those eyes, everything comes back into my heart that God has put into it; unexpected feelings arise from the depths of my soul. Usually I say what I planned; I often repeat myself, but it is never a game, recollection or a matter of striking attitudes. Each time I experience it all afresh, die and rise again to new life as I follow my account. It all happens as on the first day of my 'creation', as in the seconds of my conversion.

After the lecture – it would be better to call it a testimony – there are usually many questions and people don't let me go for a long time. Each time I stress how great people's need is for a meaning in life, for the living – not ideologized – God and for experience.

And how ashamed I was later of my sense of defeat, my contempt for people among whom there are also those whom I shall never forget. For example, a married couple, Gabriella and Stefan, devote their whole lives to the task of seeking out the most unfortunate and lonely people in hospitals and old people's homes. They give their all, soul, body and possessions, to help these people. That is not easy, but both give off a glow, as though they were still young, as though they were walking on air. These two know neither anxieties nor contentment; nor do they have any ties. From morning to evening their thought is directed towards how they can please God. (When by contrast I look at my life, it consists of sheer contentment: books, thoughts, art, prayer – they are all contentment.) Such encounters have already been granted me in the West, encounters with people who belong wholly to God. How much power, spiritual nourishment they give me!

20 July 1983

I spoke to a conference of Catholics in Linz. After the lecture, as usual many people thronged round me, asked questions and told me about themselves. I had been standing there for a long time talking to them when I saw an old nun who was waiting quietly and patiently till it was her turn to say something to me. A young minister stopped me just as it was time for me to go to the station so as not to miss my train and said, 'Someone here wants to say a couple of words to you.' With tears in her eyes the nun came up and said that she had been praying every day for forty years for the conversion of Russia and today she had now finally heard from a living witness that so many people were finding God in Russia in such a marvellous way.

And I thought: my unexpected conversion, the return of my friends to the church, all that was no coincidence. And not only the prayers of the Russian martyrs, not only their blood were the seed of our Christianity but also the prayers of all those who, like this nun, had heard the call of the Mother of God of Fatima who had prophesied to people so accurately and so lovingly that Russia would spread a diabolical doctrine in the world but would finally rise again and again become Holy Russia and the house of the All Holy Mother of God.

24 November 1983

I ask myself what I now desire more than anything else on earth. I would suddenly like to find myself back in the little wooden church which stands in the midst of a fragrant pine wood by the monastery at Riga. As always in this church I would like to feel again that I mean nothing, know nothing and can do nothing. I would like to understand not only with my head but with my whole body, until I blush for shame, how false all my thoughts have been about myself and the world. At the same time I would wish for such a joy to come over me as over the angels in heaven when they see a repentant sinner.

Then I would want irresistibly to fall on my knees and put my forehead to the warm wooden floor when the disembodied, mysteriously free voices of the nuns sing, 'Lord, I have called to you, hear me,' or when the gentle voice of the priest in the sanctuary says, 'Praise be to you for you have shown us light.' And in this gentleness there is a hidden power which can create and destroy worlds.

But if I experience this again, it will be in another world beyond.

103